NO INVESTORS?
NO PROBLEM!

A Serial Bootstrapper's Playbook
for Breakthrough Success
on a Shoestring Budget

Marty Schultz
With Judy Katz

No Investors? No Problem!

A Serial Bootstrapper's Playbook for Breakthrough Success on a Shoestring Budget.

Marty Schultz

with Judy Katz

Published by New Voices Press • 212-580-8833
Copyright © 2019 by Marty Schultz

Published in the United States

For permission to reprint material from this book, please contact Marty Schultz at marty@martyschultz.net

Library of Congress Cataloguing-in-Publication Data

No Investors? No Problem!

A Serial Bootstrapper's Playbook for Breakthrough Success on a Shoestring Budget.

Marty Schultz

with Judy Katz

ISBN 978-0-9883591-4-7

1. Entrepreneurship 2. Startups
3. Small Business and Entrepreneurship.
4. Motivational Management and Leadership.
5. Business, Motivation and Self Improvement.
6. Venture Capital 7. Strategy and Competition.

Cover design and interior graphics layout by Tony Iatridis, Innovation Design Graphics.

Additional creative editing by Kai Flanders, MFA, Creative Writing, Columbia University.

Editorial assistance and Administrative support by Layla Báez.

Dedication

This book is dedicated to Alla, my beautiful, brilliant, no-nonsense wife, who graciously puts up with my inability to tolerate boredom and makes me a better person - and a happier one - in countless ways.

This is also for Mishka - our lovely, funny, talented daughter Mariel - who shares my ability to fall asleep anywhere when we are inactive or bored. She makes me proud of her every single day.

Successfully Bootstrapped Companies at a Glance

1981 **Softbol**. We built a software converter to enable apps that only ran on expensive mini-computers to operate on the new generation of Silicon Valley microcomputers. Sold in 1989 to our largest customer.

1991 **Omtool**. We created software that automated the sending and receiving of faxes from multi-user computers, including with UNIX and Windows Server. Most of the Fortune 500 companies used our product. Initial public offering on NASDAQ (OMTL) in 1997. Sold in 2017 to Upland Software (NASDAQ: UPLD).

2000 **eSped**. We provided special education management systems to public school districts using the software-as-a-service business model. We were the largest vendor in both Texas and Massachusetts, with over 500,000 students being managed. Sold in 2016 to Frontline Education, which was owned by venture capital firm Insight Venture Partners.

2006 **McGruff SafeGuard**. We provided parental control software designed to enable parents to protect their children and teens online by monitoring their web and chat activities. Used by tens of thousands of parents. When the housing crisis and great recession of 2008 killed off an investment deal we had in place, we pivoted to keep it small and highly profitable. We continued running it as a lifestyle company until 2012.

2014 **Blindfold Games**. What started as a classroom project - when I was teaching middle school students how to design a mobile app - turned into a challenging and fun-filled commitment to creating in excess of 80 diverse, accessible mobile audio entertainment games for blind and visually impaired people of all ages. These games are currently played by over 50,000 blind people worldwide.

Table of Contents

1

Bootstrapping:

Freedom and Power in a New Age of Entrepreneurship

Your Invitation to Join Generation Bootstrap

Let's imagine you have a brilliant idea for a new start-up. You've done your research and feel confident that your concept is original, and that the consumer base is untapped. You are convinced that once you have it up and running, the marketplace is going to sit up and take notice. You know that if you capture even a tiny percentage of the millions of potential customers waiting for this new "thing," that you will, in relatively short order, be the CEO of a thriving multi-million-dollar business. Success seems to lie right around the corner.

At this point, armed with confidence and optimism, you might understandably be tempted to try to jumpstart your venture with investors' money rather than risk your own funds - which (let us assume) are limited. In fact, your relatively empty pockets would be hard-pressed to support an office, the hiring of staff, the costs of development, or the customer outreach program. This is not even taking into account the critically-important costs of marketing and promoting your new venture. Going after an investor is tempting. However, a far superior option exists: *bootstrapping.*

For the uninitiated, bootstrapping means starting a business without significant external assistance or capital. I am here to tell you that bootstrapping is one of the most effective and inexpensive ways to build your company. Bootstrapping also means less - or even no - money has to be borrowed, allowing you to retain more control over your nascent business.

***

As I write, this year has been called "Year of the Bootstrapper" by *GeekWire* Magazine. Of course, this concept cannot be confined to a single year. We have now entered into a new *era* - an era I call Generation Bootstrap. It's not an emerging trend or a passing fancy: it's an actual *movement,* one that is only gaining momentum. You may well be one of legions of young men and women today who chose to forego rising in the ranks in someone else's company, deciding instead to become a successful entrepreneur on your own terms. If so, bravo - this book is definitely for you!

Clearly, millennials are driving this movement. For one thing, too many millennials have seen a parent or grandparent who's been at the mercy of the corporate world and feel strongly the life they led is not for them. Beyond that, they as a generation are deeply committed to "doing good while doing well." They want to contribute to making life better for others. They are opting for another path by starting businesses in every sector and category. For them, going after venture capital ("VC") money is not as attractive as it used to be. In increasing numbers, they are opting to bootstrap as a contemporary alternative to dated, dusty corporate structures. Excited to be doing things their own way, they are foregoing convention to shake things up. That's the foundation we're here to build on - by examining the very best strategies and tools of bootstrapping.

I'm somewhat of a bootstrapping expert, having bootstrapped my way to success several times, so it's not surprising to me or those people who know me that I'm quite excited by this movement. I am not a millennial, so perhaps I was ahead of my time. Over the last three decades we have bootstrapped and grown five companies to a combined valuation of over $300 million dollars. My efforts began in the 1980s, when a high school friend and I started our first software company. A decade later, a business partner and I created a digital messaging company which we were able to take public six years later.

Subsequently, my colleagues and I built one of the first software-as-a-service companies, and eventually sold that company in a strategic acquisition. I am still bootstrapping, having developed a new project called **Blindfold Games**. This app development company builds audio games for the blind and visually impaired. It has led me to yet another exciting venture, **ObjectiveEd**, an educational tech company for students with many different kinds of disabilities that I will tell you about later in the book.

Frankly, along the way I have made tons of rookie mistakes that I am here to help you avoid. I learned the hard way what I needed to do, and also what to not do. Let me say from the start that to me there are no failures. I prefer to think of those mistakes as (somewhat painful) lessons that have helped me avoid future pitfalls. One of those lessons - perhaps the biggest one - was to not take investor's money before building your own foundation. "First things first," as they say.

Investor Danger

As I said before, investment money can be very tempting, but it can also be a mirage. Investors - be they angels, venture capitalists, banks, hedge funds, institutional investors or any other entity with professional capital to invest - aren't looking to help out a budding entrepreneur. They are all looking for the Next Big Thing, the next "Unicorn." Are you a unicorn? Do you have a potentially disruptive technology, product or service to offer that could make you and everyone on your team rich and famous? Look - you just might have what it takes. Nevertheless, taking on investors to find that out for certain is a big mistake. You will learn the hard and expensive way.

If you watch the television show Shark Tank, you know that investors ask very tough questions, such as: *How much of your own money have you put in? How many of the products have you sold? How many customers do you have? What is your method and cost of customers or client acquisition? You put a high valuation on your company: how did you reach that projected valuation?* Potential investors become highly critical and disinterested if your company has not yet sold much of anything to anyone. Self-confidence is great, but please understand that it will take you only so far.

Again, for argument's sake, let's say you do take your untested, unproven product or service into the world of investors, hoping that your personality, professional training and background, and of course your steadfast confidence in your burgeoning business, will "catch a whale" - meaning a major investor. Of course, you can try to do this. Many new entrepreneurs do.

My high school friend and business partner Mark and I did ask our mentor to help us get an investor for our first company, and he did. But this investor insisted we use his choice for CEO to watch over us and give us advice. When we met the prospective CEO, we thought he was too old (I think he was in his mid 50's), that he knew nothing about software (his former company put telephone and electrical wires into buildings), and, most importantly, we were too proud and bull-headed to tolerate a babysitter. We turned down the investment and decided to bootstrap.

As a result, through trial and error, we discovered which paths were dangerous to go down and the right ways to boot-strap. Our "what to not do's" can be your GPS, helping you navigate your way to using bootstrapping as a successful strategy.

If you do spend some of your valuable time pitching new business to venture capitalists, understand too that it is not the same as trying to sell a product or service. Here you are trying to raise capital for shares of an idea or concept. The blunt truth about seeking opinions from professional investors is that raising money may actually guarantee failure rather than success. I can't say this strongly enough: the only time you want to raise money is when you don't really need it - or at least not desperately. We've built our businesses by coming up with an idea, turning that idea into a profitable company, and *then* selling that company to another company.

Often, in this book, I'll use the term "we" – it was never just me but rather me and my trusted partners, working together, that made all this possible. As I've said, I've done this five times, and I'm still at it. Instead of thinking about raising money, think about your own abilities and ideas – it can lead you to success!

Let me give you a real look at what raising money entails. Do you have a clear idea of what investors expect? Seriously: angel groups and venture capital firms expect a ratio return on their investment of between 10:1 and 20:1 over several very short years.

Is your company going to be worth $500 M?

Date	Money Raised	Valuation When Money is Raised	Required Valuation in 2-4 Years
2018	$500,000	$1,000,000	$5,000,000
2020	$2,000,000	$5,000,000	$50,0000,000
2023	$10,000,000	$50,000,000	$500,000,000
2027		$500,000,000	Exit

If you raise half-a-million dollars, your company better be worth at least $5M in about two years. Your investors expect you to spend money so fast that you'll need to raise more money in your second round, and even more in your third round. If you intend to solicit funding from so-called angels, you better be sure your company is on track to be worth half-a-billion dollars.

You may wonder why venture capitalists need a 20:1 return. That's easy: out of the 20 companies a VC will invest in, with luck *one* may be successful. The others - 95 percent of them - will either be shut down when they run out of cash or become "zombie" companies - not bad enough to shut down, but certainly not salable.

Now let's consider how unique your business plan is, and what the likelihood is of your being able to raise capital. You may have heard of GUST Launch (Gust.com). It's a website that business founders use when starting a company. GUST Launch helps you through the steps needed to organize your company in preparation for raising money. Right now, there are over 75,000 companies registered on GUST Launch that have businesses focused on the Internet. Do you think there are 75,000 unique business ideas that will each one day be worth half-a-billion dollars? That's what *Facebook* was worth three years after it started. Or will there possibly be 15,000, 5,000, or even 1,000 companies that might meet that criteria?

Let's assume that there are 1,000 unique business ideas that will be worth half-a-billion dollars. Suppose your company is among that 1,000 that have real potential. What's the chance of your company being funded by outside investors? Regardless of how wonderful your idea seems to you, there are probably 999 other people out there - possibly all registered on GUST Launch - who have similar ideas. And only one or two in this group will get funded.

If your goal is raising money, here's what you can expect:

- It will take six months.
- Your business will be entirely on hold during that time.
- If you fail to get funded you've lost at least six months.

When I was trying to raise money in Miami for one of my companies, I pitched some Boston-based venture capitalists. Many knew of me, and several said yes, but with one condition: move the company from Miami to Boston. I asked why.

You know what they said? Without any sugar-coating or mincing their words, they said: "When we *replace* you, we'll need a new CEO. We only know CEOs who live in Boston. And we're not going to waste *our* money moving *your* company." So, if you do raise outside money, guess what:

- You're now an employee, answering to someone else.
- If you disagree with their plans, you could be outvoted.
- If you mess up, you may be fired.

To recap:

- Your idea must grow into a half-a-billion-dollar company.
- 95% of all funded companies are headed for failure.
- You've wasted 6 months or more if you don't get financing.

***

Bootstrapping Basics

We're about to embark on a long journey together. Over the course of the next eleven chapters I'm going to break down each and every aspect of the bootstrapping process. By the time you finish reading this book *you* will have the toolkit needed to rise above the crowd. Before we begin on our journey, it will be useful to have an overview of the road we're about to travel in the following chapters. So here is what you are about to discover:

Chapter 2. Passion, Creativity and Persistence: Potent Combination for Eliminating Obstacles. Passion is primary. Creativity and persistence are what makes the difference between success and failure. Here I show you how desperation and being faced with failure forced me to be creative and persistent in order to find mentors, take vacations, get into grad school at no cost, and close major deals.

Chapter 3. Be the Aspirin: Solving Their Pain is the Best Way to Grow. Looking back over hobbies that evolved into businesses since I was a young teen, from photography to food delivery to software, I analyze why solving a customer's pain - knowing what they really need, even f they themselves may not - is the critical component of any business.

Chapter 4. Talking: Make the Whole World Your Focus Group and Network. In this chapter I explain why not talking to your potential customers will doom you to failure - or as I prefer to describe it - will earn you a hard lesson. Here I show you the importance of getting the right feedback from the right people, and illustrate this example with a description of a language app I tried to launch in the 1980's. I thought it was a billion-dollar idea that would revolutionize the computer industry but failed to test it with customers.

Chapter 5. Stumble. Fall. Get Up. Do it Again. A New Take on 'Failure.' Here I dissect each of my "failures" - including what should have been a highly successful app to teach math, and a private jet charter website akin to "Kayak.com." These examples will show you how to know if your venture is heading for failure and when, why and how to bail out.

Chapter 6. Mentor Connect: Why You Need Them and They Need You. This chapter will demonstrate that, early on, while I was being mentored, I had no idea what my mentors were trying to accomplish. From one that would only talk to me by grunting to another who always stiffed me with the bill at lunch, they taught me important entrepreneurial lessons that enabled me to find other mentors and eventually become an effective mentor myself.

Chapter 7. When to Hire? After You Learn How to Do It Yourself. Here you see how my having to call up a customer week after week - begging them to finally pay for the product they bought over six months ago - taught me what "accounts receivable and collections" is all about. However, as I explain, learning every aspect of your business doesn't mean doing everything yourself: I've met so many amazingly talented people by giving them a chance to prove themselves and teach me how their job should be done.

Chapter 8. Pivoting: What You Must Do When It's Simply Not Working. Pivot means to "rotate, turn, re-volve, spin, swivel, twirl, whirl, wheel, oscillate." Here we discuss the all-important turnaround.   In business, our customers or potential customers tell us when a pivot was needed in many ways - but initially, I too often ignored their advice. In one company, our pivot was to abandon our original 'big idea" that was designed to help businesses and ended up bringing McGruff "The Crime Dog" (remember the slogan "Take a Bite out of Crime"?) into the digital age but to a very different and much more receptive audience.

Chapter 9. Lasering in: Focus on the Short-Term or Risk Failure. In this chapter we see how easy - and dangerous - it is to put your focus on those bright, shiny long-term hopes and dreams when growing a company. To illustrate, I go through several of the mistakes we made by *not* staying focused on the short-term, and also how to determine if a new opportunity is worth pursuing. One thing is certain: as long as you make fewer mistakes than your competitors, in the long run your company may well end up winning.

Chapter 10. Small Budget Big Impact: Guerilla Market-ing Tactics. This is a fun chapter in which I report on how an inflatable rhino the size of a UPS truck was just one of the ways in which we used guerilla marketing tactics to get our brand known and acquire customers without spending money we honestly didn't have. I discuss the reasons behind each of our tactics and the brainstorming that went into them; you can garner ideas on how to implement your own guerilla strategies.

Chapter 11. The Winding Road That Led to Blindfold Games. Life is full of surprises, which is what makes it fun - with bootstrapping a major element in what makes business fun - for me, and hopefully soon for you, too. In this chapter I describe how what began as an after-school club to teach my daughter's class how to design an iPhone app ended up improving the lives of tens of thousands of blind and visually impaired people. I talk about a kerfuffle I had with Apple's App Store, and how, by always doing the right thing, your company and your customers will benefit in the long term.

Chapter 12. Following My Own Rules and Launching ObjectiveEd. In this final chapter I describe our newest bootstrapped company, **ObjectiveEd**. Our company's mission is to maximize the educational outcome for the millions of students with disabilities through artificial intelligence, gamified education and closed-loop progress reporting.

As we wind up this first chapter, there is one more cautionary note that I cannot emphasize enough. Entrepreneurship is not for everyone. If your goal is simply to make a lot of money or run a big company, please don't start your own venture. If you do start your venture, you'll find yourself working at least 80 hours per week, making very little money (at first), and will be met with constant frustration. However, if your goal is to change the world, or follow your passion, I can tell you that nothing will ever be as satisfying.

At the end of each chapter there is a short list of takeaways from that chapter: specific *Do's* and *Don'ts*. For this chapter those key takeaways are:

- **Understand your personal goals before starting a company.**
- **Raising outside money won't guarantee success; it may even guarantee failure.**
- **Be passionate, creative and persistent.**

Now that I've laid out our roadmap you should be ready to begin. Take a deep breath, turn the page, and *let's start bootstrapping*!

***

2

Passion, Creativity and Persistence:

A Potent Combination for Eliminating Obstacles

I assume you are passionate about becoming an entrepreneur or you would not be reading this book. Passion *is* the first prerequisite for success - and it is only the beginning. Creativity and persistence are two other major ingredients you'll need to power you down the road that leads to an accomplished business.

The main source of frustration that I hear about from struggling entrepreneurs is not being able to elicit attention. "My business could make an impact if I could just get my foot in the door with so-and-so," they complain. Disheartened by seeming disinterest and setbacks, these entrepreneurs often become convinced that their lack of connections is the main factor blocking their path. They see themselves as banging on a closed door which, if somehow opened to them, would lead to a gleaming world filled with amazing opportunities, exciting partnerships and lucrative handshake deals.

While it is certainly true that connections and partnerships are incredibly important in business - as in life - this be-all and end-all conclusion is faulty. Influential people who can help you do not exist behind a secret door to which ordinary people will never find the key. Of course, nobody gets to where they are without at least a little help from those who have already made it. But talented and successful people *do* want to give back, to further promising work, and also because they too have had such help at various points in their own careers and business growth. They are more than willing to help those who demonstrate potential and drive. However, they need to know you are worth their time - that you are a serious self-starter. It is up to *you*, and no one else, to demonstrate this to them.

Mentors *are* out there. I will go into much more detail on how I found mine, and how I mentor others these days, in a later chapter. For now, let's concentrate on the fact that when bootstrapping your business, obstacles will pop up as you try to get your foot in various doors. The more competitive your industry, the more obstacles you will face. The key to overcoming them is being creative in how you approach and overcome obstacles, and then persisting in the face of repeated setbacks. Creativity and persistence are the two most valuable tools in my professional arsenal, and they are especially important to someone just starting out. In the early days of your business, you'll use these traits, time and time again, to problem-solve your challenges.

To me, creativity shows us that there is no such thing as an obstacle - there is always a more unique way to get from one place to the other. The commonly accepted path might be a waste of time, or just not right for you, and you will often need to think of something different. Persistence then comes into play: it's the never-quit attitude that gives you the strength and resolve to try enough new strategies and ideas until you find the one that puts you on the right path. Together these forces are a potent combination to get under, around, over or through any barrier that shows up on that bumpy road to fulfilling your passionately conceived, ambitious and close-to-your-heart business venture.

In this chapter I'm going to show you how I used creativity and persistence to get myself hired for a first job in my field, got to participate in important meetings, was able to stand out from the crowd, proved my resourcefulness when the chips were down, and willed myself to succeed. The chapter is divided into five sections. Each contains a story or stories conveying a lesson from my long and diverse career.

As you will see, not every story is a tale of success. Often a failure can convey just as much wisdom. You may be taken aback by my boldness in some situations, but in my opinion being bold is a form of risk, and taking risks is something every good entrepreneur must do. Not every gamble will work out, but when the right one does your life will change. That's the message of this chapter, which in sum is "Dare to be Great." I know that inside you is the power to become daring, intrepid, and tenacious enough to turn your dreams into reality. As my stories show, it won't be easy, but if you're like me then you also love a challenge, and you also know that the highest branches bear the sweetest fruit.

***

Assert Your Ability

Taking a journey back through some of those moments when creativity and persistence advanced my career, it makes sense to start with my first real job. As a kid, I was never interested in having a paper route, which I saw as a waste of time with minimal reward. During my freshman year in high school I was a bored, restless intelligent kid who had nowhere to put his energy. I'm sure many young entrepreneurs can relate to that feeling - an abundance of vitality and intensity with no container to put it into. Nothing really excited me until my sophomore year of high school, when I discovered computers and became passionate about them. That moment everything changed. When one of my friends told me that you could skip regular classes in order to learn computing, I found a sort of home. Suddenly I could cut boring old history class to play with what looked like space-age devices. I had found something infinitely more interesting.

Spending all my free time in the lab, I quickly became an expert hacker, reveling in all I discovered could be done in that arena. By junior year, I was far and away the best hacker in the school. Then, at the beginning of that year, the computer center announced that they were looking for a new IT manager. It was a position always given to a senior, and I was a mere junior, but I knew I had to have that job. I made up my mind to *get* that job, no matter how tough it would be.

I realized that the traditional application process wouldn't give me the chance I needed, so I decided to contact the manager of the computer center, Jerry Damm, directly. I called him up, and the first words out of my mouth were: "I'm the best hacker in the school. That means I can stop anyone *else* from getting into your system." That was enough to get me an interview. When I showed up, I must admit I was a little intimidated: Jerry was chain-smoking cigarettes and looked at me like I was something distasteful he had long forgotten in his refrigerator. I steeled myself against my nerves and gave him a demonstration of my abilities.

Jerry put out his cigarette and looked me over. "Can you

really make sure nobody breaks into this computer?" he asked, gauging my confidence level.

Computer center at my first job.

"Absolutely," I answered. "Since I can hack better than any of them, there's no way they can get in."

That was that: I had my first job - and what a dream job it was. I brought my friends in, and we all got to hang out in an amazing computer center every day, teaching ourselves new things, competing with each other, and pushing our intellectual limits. In retrospect, I probably would not have had so many extremely positive things in my future life if I hadn't boldly asserted my ability to Jerry. I showed him why I was different - why I had something nobody else could bring to the table. Then I worked hard to prove myself to indeed be an invaluable asset. I can tell you that no student ever hacked into the computer on my watch!

The lesson here, which I learned early on, is that if you want to truly succeed in business you need to assert your ability to the point where it becomes undeniable. I could have told myself: *They only give the position to seniors* and given up, in much the same way that people tell themselves: *That company only hires or does business with people they already know.* The truth is that nobody will pass up true talent after you show them how working with you can solve their problems - and I did solve a potential problem for this computer center manager. When you have the opportunity to take charge of a situation, put your best foot forward and do not be afraid to lead with a clear and honest explanation of what is different and valuable about you.

Naturally, in order to do that well you first need to ask your-self: "What differentiates me from every other bright-eyed hopeful that walks through the doors of power?" In business terms, whether it is a meeting with a distributor who might pick up your product, a developer who you can convince to work for you, or a one-on-one with a CEO who can become a mentor, you *must* show them that you not only have what it takes, but that you have something totally unique that no one else can give them. If you can do that you are sure to get that all important "yes" when you need it most - and not because they want to give it to you, but because you've offered them the smartest choice for their business. Give them no choice but to offer you a chance. Then take that chance and knock it out of the park.

***

Do First, Ask Later

As I said, my high school computer center proved to be an early training center for learning sound business lessons. Another lesson was learned when my friends and I were suddenly faced with a complex technical problem and decided to troubleshoot it all on our own. These 1970's computers had big disk drives that had to be inserted into large storage units that looked like giant washing machines. Each of the disk drives contained "platters" - circular disks the size of dinner plates on which magnetic data was stored in a disk drive. Disk drives from this era typically had about twenty platters. These were all mounted on the same spindle, which was then inserted into the "washing machine."

One day, one of these "platters" out of the twenty in the stack had a defect and could no longer store information on it. My friends and I were determined to fix it by ourselves, without consulting the powers that be - as of course we should have. In truth, as teenagers, we didn't have much regard for the powers that be. Besides, we figured we were the smartest kids in school - if *we* couldn't figure it out who could?

We gave it a shot, were sure we fixed it, and congratulated ourselves on our brilliant ingenuity. When we turned that machine back on it began making horrible clunking noises. Within five minutes we were now sure we had completely destroyed this forty-thousand-dollar computer disk drive. Panicked, we had to call in a technician who oversaw the computer center's equipment. It didn't take long for this expert to figure out that we had tried to fix it on our own. Even though I thought I would get fired, I admitted my actions. I was a renegade but not a liar.

Fortunately, the tech was able to fix it and covered for us. We had gotten lucky, but the lesson I learned that day was not what you might expect. It was *not* to be cautious. In fact, just the opposite. It was: *Do first, ask later*, which became a sort of creed of mine. Even though I did screw up, I still had gained valuable experience by trying to fix that computer disk drive - something the authorities would never have let me try on my own. The plain fact is that if you ask permission, people will generally say no. If you go ahead and do it, all you have to do is own up to it and apologize. Of course, I am not giving you carte blanche permission to do anything criminal - just to be bold.

That attitude can work in your favor when you are starting your own company. Don't be afraid to make bold plays and do things others might consider outrageous. Even if they backfire you will learn from your mistakes, others will admire your gumption, and if you pull it off, you will leapfrog past your meeker-minded competitors.

There was yet another important lesson I learned that day: always read the instruction manual before attempting something reckless. It was something we neglected to do and should have done. As we discovered afterwards, on the very first page of that disk drive's manual it stressed: *do not disassemble the disk stack!* Well, you live, and you learn. Still, once again, I don't regret my boyhood incautiousness for one minute, since it helped teach me to take risks. I have no argument with manuals, but sometimes the best thing you can do is throw the manual out of the window - after reading it, of course.

The final lesson I learned from that experience was to take responsibility for my actions. Sure, I had done something stupid, but I wasn't dishonest about it and I didn't try to push the blame off on my friends or on the equipment. Jerry Damm respected me for that, and I respected myself. There's almost nothing you can do that can't be forgiven (short of murder), but people will call you out in an instant if you lie to them. Even when you make mistakes, keep your character intact, and more often than not you will be given the benefit of the doubt. In this case, I got to keep my job and the respect of all my friends. Always be prepared to fall on your sword - it won't cut as deeply as you might think.

***

Reach Out Proactively to Key Players

Now I'm going to tell you something about me that may be surprising: I was once given a full-ride scholarship to the best veterinary medicine school in the country, namely Cornell. Sounds a bit strange for an entrepreneur, but I have always been the type to try my hand at many different things. Actually, if I didn't have that inherent characteristic, I doubt I would have ever found myself developing a gaming application for the blind!

At the point in my life when I was offered the scholarship, I had just finished a Masters in Cognitive Psychology at Carnegie-Mellon. Looking for a new challenge, I heard my sister's husband say that it was nearly impossible to get accepted into a veterinary school in the United States. He had tried, failed, and ended up studying to be a veterinarian at a Belgian university. I was young and always ready for a challenge, so I thought: "Why not?" and I set my sights on getting into Cornell, which had the best vet program in the country.

First thing I did was to enroll in Pharmacology courses as part of my studies in graduate school. Then I began doing something just as important: researching the names of the professors of the Admissions Committee of the Vet School at Cornell!

One professor had his information listed publicly. I contacted him, asking him to please send me his research. He had studied the lactation behaviors of sheep in Australia, and written papers on how to use hormone therapy to convince a female sheep to give milk to another sheep's offspring.

In truth, I had very little interest in the habits of female Australian sheep. But that wasn't what I was after: I was after a *connection*. I carefully read through the professor's papers to see if I could find other experiments that he could do to extend his concept further. I kept working on it continuously until I had enough information to write a letter to him. I would never conduct any of these experiments myself, but I was wooing him, showing him that I believed what he was doing was important, and asserting that I would be an excellent addition to his team. I knew the only way I would gain admission to that college was to have someone like him help get me in. I needed to have him respect me and want me to work with him.

Within a few months of back-and-forth correspondence with this professor, my actions got me the offer of a fellowship in the combined Animal Science and Veterinary program at Cornell. I was not only accepted into the program but given a full-ride scholarship!

I only stayed at Cornell for one year, since being a veterinarian was not my path, but I had proven to myself that I could get into an "impossible" program. More than that, I also learned a lesson that would serve me well in all the rest of my endeavors, namely: *don't be afraid to reach out to the people in charge and impress them by knowing all about their work*. Put them - and you - in a good light and make yourself known to them.

This lesson can be directly applied to your entrepreneurial endeavors. Reach out to mentors proactively and tell them what you admire about them or their work. Don't be afraid of rejection - nobody will get mad at receiving an email showing respect for their accomplishments. More often than not you will establish a connection, one that may serve you for years to come. It may not be your ticket to the big-time, but it can be another step that helps pave your way on the path to success. Every stone you place on that path is extremely valuable.

***

Blow Them Away with Your Tenacity

Let me ask you a series of questions. What would you do if you needed to speak to someone in your field - someone who could really help you in the development of your business - but you didn't know that person at all? What if all you have is their address and phone number? How far would you go to make that connection? How creative are you willing to be in order to get an audience with them? How persistent would you be in the face of possible or even probable rejection?

Whatever your answer, I'm guessing it won't be quite as extreme as the two stories I'm about to relate. Thirty-five years ago, my best friend from high school and I were in the process of launching a software company we named **Softbol**. I knew I could use prominent, knowledgeable, and well-connected advisors to help with execution and development. Coincidently, I had heard from a colleague about the recent retirement of a man who had been a Vice President for a major computer maker and his background was relevant for our company. Let's call him Jake. I had never met Jake, but other people told me he would be a great advisor.

This was before the Internet - before email, before texting, before cell phones, before voicemail and even before answering machines. There were only three ways to reach people back then: a phone call to their landline at home, a letter via US Mail, or a visit to their home.

I managed to find Jake's phone number and home address, but that was all I had to go on - there were no direct connections to introduce us. I started to phone Jake at his home and did so every day for a month. I never got through.

Did I give up? I think you know the answer. I knew I had to be super-creative in order to get around the communication obstacles. I knew I could not simply show up at his front door – that would be an invasion of privacy. Instead, I sat down to plan out my next move and decided to arrange for a flower shop delivery of a houseplant to his residence, along with a flattering note. And that's what I did.

The day my plant arrived my phone rang. It was Jake, eager to talk to me - impressed by my determination. He even invited us to lunch, where he gave us valuable advice that we were able to use to help get our company off the ground. Happily retired, he stopped short of agreeing to be a regular advisor on my project, but that meeting gave me confidence in this strategy. If you don't have easy access to someone, find a way to make them available to you through whatever means necessary - even if those means turn out to be a surprise houseplant. My creativity was key here. No problem should be so big that you can't creatively figure out how to get past it.

Another story that confirms this lesson happened to me a bit later in life, during my time working on the **McGruff SafeGuard** family safety project, which I will describe in depth later. We had bootstrapped the project as far as we could go, and by this time we were seeking outside funding.

Just as we were about to close an investment deal, one of the venture capitalists - an investor from New York named Steve - got cold feet and pulled the Term Sheet. Of course, we were disappointed, but instead of giving up we jumped into action. The very next morning, at 5 AM no less, my partner Dave and I took a flight from Miami for a surprise visit to Steve's offices in New York. We had no meeting scheduled: we just waited for him to arrive at his office and sat outside nervously for two hours until he finally walked through the doors.

When he showed up, Steve was so blown away by our tenacity that he resumed negotiations, and we left with a handshake deal. Even if Steve hadn't confirmed his investment, I would never have regretted getting on that flight. It was the best thing we could have done in the situation, and the best thing we could have done for our company. You have to *always* be ready to take that crucial step out into the unknown, to "give it your all" for your project. If people see how far you are willing to go for your venture, they will feed off your energy, and in most cases be willing to give you the help you need. You need to believe in yourself enough to hop on that plane.

***

Know What They Need and Then Hit the Pavement

My last anecdote for this chapter - lots more in the chapters ahead - describes what was probably one of my zaniest endeavors. It was back in 1982. I was feeling a bit burned out and desperately needed a vacation but couldn't afford one of any consequence. I loved Jamaica, in the West Indies, but I certainly didn't want (nor could I afford) to pay premium resort prices. Then a friend told me that people on the island needed hard goods. I knew there were a lot of bars in the area, so that meant they might need blenders and coolers. I also thought the smaller hotels might need small fans, which were not readily available in that part of the world at that time.

On a whim I bought a large ice chest and filled it with blenders and fans and then booked a flight. I walked through Jamaican Customs with such confidence that they didn't look twice at my haul. I also didn't call anyone before going down there and didn't make any kind of hotel reservation. I was doing an experiment in real-time: could I get a vacation by bartering goods?

Turns out I could.

I took a taxi from the airport in Montego Bay to the town of Negril, and then stashed all my stuff at a bar. Negril wasn't very developed, especially as you headed away from the center of town. It was filled with small hotels that had maybe five or ten rooms. The restaurants were independent spots – mainly small Tiki huts - with maybe ten seats set around a bar. Walking up and down the streets, I stopped to talk to people to see who might want to do a deal with me. As it turned out, the proper question wasn't who would take the deal - I had such interest that it was more who could give me the *best* deal for the goods I brought with me. I ended up trading the ice chest itself for a four-night stay at a beachside hotel. My next deal was a table-top fan for several meals. This successful bartering went on and on. I had the best vacation of my life.

This story is funny, but for our purposes it also has a deeper context. By researching what my potential "customers" needed, I was able to provide an "aspirin" (fans and blenders) for their "pain" (inability to obtain critically-needed import-ed products due to a malfunctioning government). I explore pain and aspirins in the next chapter, but this Jamaican bartering adventure was a win-win situation for all of us: I obtained a room or a dinner that cost me very little money—essentially just the cost of the equipment I bartered—and they improved their business with a very modest outlay.

Do your homework! Always know your audience before you go into a negotiation. If you have something they don't have and which they deeply desire, they will be highly moti-vated to make a deal. Do this and you might get something far more significant than my vacation: you might get yourself the deal of a lifetime.

Also, don't be afraid to look in unexpected places for cli-ents, partners, or investors. In that little travel experience, my Jamaican "partners" were some of the nicest people I ever met, and some of them became more like friends than business partners. Certainly those "deals" reaped some of the most enjoyable rewards. I can tell you that I came home fully refreshed and ready to "kick ass" in my next business venture - or, as I like to think of it - my next business *ad-venture.* As I've said before and will say again, having fun is the main reason I do anything. Interestingly, the money often follows.

The world will always present you with obstacles. What matters is how you respond to them. That's where your passion comes in. Then, if you employ those two additional traits - creativity and persistence - nothing, and I do mean nothing, can block your path to success.

But of course, there are more lessons ahead.

***

Key takeaways:

- Be assertive about your abilities, but do it based on real skills.

- Always read the manual before attempting something stupid.

- Do try to fix things first, and then get permission.

- Own up to your mistakes and throw yourself on the mercy of others.

- Find out who the key players are, then reach out to them in inventive ways.

- Be tenacious in everything you do.

- Don't be afraid to do something unusual to attract your prospect's attention.

- Take risks. You'll be glad you did.

- Look for opportunities in unexpected places.

3

Be the Aspirin:

Solving Their Pain is the Best Way to Grow

When bootstrapping a business, you need to ask yourself some initial questions that, properly answered, will ultimately determine the success of your endeavor. The first question should be: *Is my company addressing a "pain" that people have?* I like to think of entrepreneurship as creative problem-solving. The complexities of business, and of course life itself, regularly create a series of challenges for each of us. If we want to develop a successful venture right from the starting gate, it's up to us to identify and solve those business challenges. Far too often people misunderstand the problem they are trying to solve, and as a result come up with the wrong solution. I have made this mistake more than once, which is why I know that this is a seemingly obvious but often overlooked skill-set for the fledgling entrepreneur.

The first thing you have to do is understand *exactly* where the customer's pain is. If you don't properly comprehend what they need help with, there is no way you can convince them to spend money with you. No matter how wonderful you think your idea is, if you aren't solving someone's pain, no one will care. Believe me: *everyone* has some sort of pain they want help with. That's the reality of business, and of the human condition - people are always looking to solve something. That solution should come from you! If you are smart and intuitive enough you will learn how to identify and solve a great many problems along the way for potential customers. You just have to be incredibly prescient in how you go about it.

Think of this pain/aspirin concept as a form of leverage - you need to intuit what to bring to the table. Your customers aren't going to tell you what's wrong with them. Why would they? They don't know you, and they certainly aren't interested in giving you their money unless they think they have to. It's your job to make them think that if they don't use your product or service their pain is going to grow to the point where it becomes unmanageable.

It may be useful to think of this concept as a visit to the doctor's office. You are the doctor and the customer is the patient. A patient doesn't come in and properly diagnose himself. He doesn't have the capability to say: "I have arthritis." Instead he'll say: "My bones ache, especially when it's cold outside." It's up to you to put together the information and form a diagnosis. The first thing you, as the doctor, will do is ask what's bothering him. Then you will run a series of "tests" to see which external factors are causing the symptoms. Finally, you will give him your best determination of what his health problem is, and how you will resolve it so he can heal.

Incidentally, just to add to this medical analogy, in today's world many people will go to the Internet, research their symptoms, and give you *their* diagnosis. In business as in medicine, part of what you will be faced with as the aspirin will be correcting their inaccurate self-diagnosis and showing them your expertise in pinpointing where their pain truly originates and how you can make it go away.

As you can see, it is the same in business. Like the doctor, you will have to sit down and talk to those in your customer base. You will have to become an expert at finding out what their real challenges are, because, again, *they may not even know.* You have to talk with them about ways their business-es, and perhaps their lives, too, could be improved, uncover ways they may be wasting valuable time, and show them which things may be causing them the most aggravation.

Once you understand what the customer needs and isn't getting you will be ready to ask yourself the second vital question all entrepreneurs must ask: *What kind of a pill (solution) can I offer that will alleviate this pain?* Keep in mind that, more often than not, your business will be addressing *multiple* pains, and you may need to offer a particular cus-tomer more than one type of aspirin.

Throughout the three sections of this chapter I am going to show you ways in which I have made this concept work throughout my career. I will also reveal to you some ways in which ignoring it caused me to fail. As I mentioned before, I am not crazy about the word *fail,* because to me failure is often truly an ideal lesson in how to stop doing something the wrong way so you can pivot and do it right. Incidentally, both failure and pivoting are important topics we will exam-ine in detail in later chapters.

The three stories I am about to reference occurred in different eras of my life. They each offer a prime example of how finding the pain and solving it, correctly applied, can lead to success. It's a formula you will be able to apply again and again - a new way of looking at the world that has the power to transform problems into solutions.

***

Make Sure A Pain Actually Exists

I was thirteen and fascinated by cameras. I've always been into technical machines with a lot of moving parts, so it makes sense that in my adolescent development cameras preceded computers. Back then I had a fifty-dollar 35mm camera with a bunch of lenses. This was in 1968, when color film was available but also extremely expensive, and most people couldn't develop color film at home. For me it was all about black and white film.

Around this time, I had my first flash of what I thought was a brilliant business plan: I would take pictures of the outside of my neighbors' houses and sell those photos to them. My idea was that homeowners would naturally want a beautiful black and white picture of their homes, in part because it was snow season, and I thought I could make the pictures look good from an artistic viewpoint. Why would people not want pictures of where they lived, where they raised their kids, where they spent so much of their time?

With these convictions in mind, I began bootstrapping my very first business. I would take a picture of a house, develop it into an 8 by 10 photo, go back and wait until the family got home, then try to sell it to them for five dollars. I had proactively taken the pictures, hoping to anticipate a need they didn't even know they had. On cruise lines and at theme parks, there are often roving photographers who take your picture as you enjoy some activity that memorializes your vacation, hoping the photo itself will entice you to buy it. In retrospect, that's what I was trying to do with my photographs.

I made only one sale. So, still determined to not lose my investment, I began to leave pictures with families overnight, and then go back the next day hoping they would have grown attached to them. In the end, all I got were a lot of polite "No Thank You's."

Looking back, I know why this venture failed: there was no pain there. One of the things I should have done was to conduct some preliminary research, asking a few neighbors if they even *wanted* a picture of their house. If I had done that, I would have realized that I was trying to solve a pain they didn't have. More importantly, I might have been able to identify a *different* problem they might want solved. They might have said: "I don't need a picture of my house, but my daughter needs headshots for an acting class."

With fifty years hindsight, what I also could have done was arrange to take pictures not just of the outside of the house but of the *family* standing in front of their house. That very likely would have had more value to the homeowners. You can't sell something to someone unless there is an *emotional* attachment.

Realistically, I should have started this process by simply asking my parents if they wanted a picture of our *own* home. They probably would have said no. But I was young, bullhead-ed, and wanted to see this happen, so I figured, "I'm just going to go out there and take the pictures first. These pictures are so good that people will want to buy them." I didn't realize that people don't spend money on things unless they absolutely need them, or they really want them. Again - and I can't say this enough - your customers have to be in some sort of pain.

When bootstrapping a business, it is vital to listen to your customers in a deeply intuitive way. Before you sink tons of time, effort and money into your business, make sure you fully understand your customer - perhaps understand them better than they understand themselves. If you gain that insight, you're sure to see what pains them, and come up with the right medicine for it.

***

Aspirins in Unlikely Places

Not long after the demise of my photo business, I initiated another early entrepreneurial experience: one involving my high school cafeteria. If there was one place where pain existed, it was in the high school cafeteria of the 1970s. The pizza tasted like cardboard, the meat was a mysterious grey color, and don't get me started on the "chop suey." I still didn't understand the concept of pain and aspirin, but my friends and I really disliked the food. I knew how to drive, and my parents let me use their very old car to drive to school every day. Why not, at lunch break, drive to McDonalds with my two friends? We did, and we bought Big Macs and fries, then enjoyed our great meal in the lunch cafeteria. All the other teens were jealous.

Who wouldn't prefer McDonalds?

Within a week a few teens approached me and asked if I could get them lunch as well. I was getting lunch for about seven people and word began to spread around the school. In today's lingo, my 1970's version of UberEATS was "going viral."

In retrospect, I had found a pain: the awful food in the cafeteria that everyone hated, and I had identified the aspirin: McDonalds and Burger King. My best friends and I "bootstrapped" a food delivery service, charging students a small fee to free them from the misery of bad lunches.

Each morning I utilized a small computer program I set up to get everyone's orders. I didn't have to do much advertising - I had identified such a large pain that there was plenty of demand. By eleven o'clock in the morning I had everything totaled up, at which point I would call McDonald's and place the order. Just as the lunch bell rang, I would drive over, pick up the orders, and then drive to the back of the school, where I received a hero's welcome as I dispensed food to my happy paying customers.

More and more customers began streaming in. I even had to create a special type of drink holder that went in the back seat of the car so I could transport twenty or more sodas without spilling. I also wrote a part of this little computer program that would keep track of people's balance if they couldn't pay me right away. Right then and there I would know what their lunch would cost, including my service fee, and they would pay me the next day.

Within a month I had fifty kids giving me orders daily. That may not seem like a lot of customers, but in high school fifty kids as regular customers is enough to get you noticed.

Guess who noticed us? It was my competition: the lunch ladies. They reported me to the school administration, and they shut me down. I felt honored, in a way, that I had become big enough to threaten their business. I was a legitimate young entrepreneur who had made waves in his marketplace - even if that marketplace was only a high school cafeteria.

This story may seem insignificant to someone who wants to start a large business, but it's certainly indicative of a model that works. I identified a problem, I implemented a creative solution, and I continued to innovate as my customer base expanded.

Another lesson I want to relate in this chapter pertains to something I learned in the early days of launching **Softbol**, the first software company that my partner Mark and I formed in the early 1981. Back then computers made by most computer companies cost at least $50,000. At the same time, the micro-computer revolution was hitting Silicon Valley, and those computer manufacturers were using new technologies to make computers that cost only $5,000. Those cheaper computers were just as powerful as the expensive ones. We identified a pain and the appropriate aspirin:

- There were lots of great software apps for big, expensive computers
- But there were **NO** software apps for the new, cheap computers: **That was the pain.**
- We were going to create a converter to move all these software apps to the new cheap computers: **That was the aspirin.**

We made an assumption that a cheap computer would be easier to sell than an expensive one, so lots of companies would use our converter to almost magically move software apps to these new inexpensive computers.

Back then, there were companies known as "computer resellers" that specialized in automating certain types of businesses.

For example, there were computer resellers that specialized in automating doctor's offices. They typ-

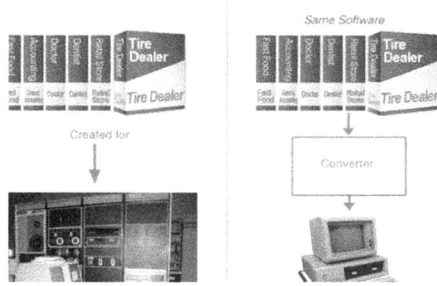

Our **Softbol** converter enabled great software apps built for expansive computers to operate on low-cost computers.

ically sold their own "doctor management" software, plus a $50,000 computer, to a doctor. Let's assume the "doctor management" software cost $20,000. The doctor would buy the entire system for $70,000 from the computer reseller.

Using our "magical" converter, that computer reseller could sell a $5,000 computer that was just as powerful, along with their own "doctor management" software to a doctor for a total of $25,000. Since that's so much cheaper, the computer reseller could theoretically sell to many more doctors. ***Our plan was to sell our converter to these resellers.***

We had started this company because I saw this as an opportunity and my gut said, "go for it." Of course, at that point I had no clue as to how to turn this idea into a business.

Remember, this was back in 1980. Microsoft was a tiny company – just 50 people. Large software companies like Google and Facebook didn't yet exist. Computer makers didn't understand how important software would become. The head of one of the largest computer makers famously said, "Why would anyone ever want a computer in their home?"

My partner Mark and I knew better. We believed our idea was revolutionary, or in today's lingo, *disruptive.* Cheap powerful computers were coming out of Silicon Valley. There were hundreds of great software apps. Almost overnight - because of our converter –software for these new inexpensive computers did become available.

In our minds, these thousands of computer resellers – experts at providing software to doctors, lawyers, gas stations, restaurants – any small business you could think of – would be using our converter. We were so confident that our idea was revolutionary that we decided it really shouldn't be cheap. We set the price at $5,000 for the starter kit and an additional $100 for each computer sold with our converter. We put together a spreadsheet to forecast our business. According to our calculations we'd be millionaires within a few years.

Did we find a pain? Yes – there was no software for the new cheap computers. Did we come up with an aspirin? Yes – we built a converter to move all those great software apps to the new cheap computers. But what we did wrong was identify who really *had* the pain. The computer resellers – the ones selling the $50,000 computers –didn't have any pain. Their businesses were perfectly viable, whether they were selling the expensive computers or the cheap ones.

The doctors also didn't really have the pain. Doctors who could afford a $50,000 computer along with $20,000 for the "doctor management" software didn't have pain. Sure, that's a lot of money. But there wasn't real pain there either.

The doctors that couldn't afford a $50,000 computer had pain. But since we were selling to resellers instead of the actual customer (the doctor), we never spoke with any of the doctors who had pain.

Our basic assumption – that the resellers would sell more because their product appealed to both rich and poor doctors – was flawed. We found out that if a reseller was selling to 10 doctors with the expensive computer, he still would only sell to 10 doctors when using our "magical" converter technology with the cheaper computer. After all, the reseller made most of his money on his $20,000 "doctor management" software.

As I said, our first mistake was to not properly identify who had the pain. And sometimes, even if you've identified a pain, you cannot cost-effectively reach those people who have that pain. Our second mistake was being dependent on someone else to grow our business. We were expecting the resellers to sell to more doctors so that our business would expand. From a macro-economic perspective, it made sense. From the perspective of each individual reseller, it was an absurd conclusion. I should have talked to dozens of re-sellers first!

Our third mistake was being fooled by our own perceptions. No one cares how great your product is or how much it's disrupting an industry. If your product does not solve someone's pain, move on.

***

Alleviate Every Pain You Find

Let's jump forward to 1991 and look at a lesson I learned at **Omtool** Corp. - a company we bootstrapped, built up, took public, and eventually sold for millions. Back then, faxing was the preferred method of communication between two businesses – for sending invoices, important letters, sales orders – anything that needed to be delivered instantly.

To give you some historical context, back in 1991 most businesses did not have Internet access, so no one could use email to send documents. Up to this point there were two ways for a business to send a document, such as an important letter, to a customer: US Mail or FEDEX. Mail took about a week, FEDEX cost about $50. Fax machines, on the other hand, were becoming popular. You just plug your fax machine into your telephone landline, put the paper into the fax machine, dial the customer's phone number, and press SEND. Magically, it pops out at the customer's fax machine, a far better solution than the alternatives.

The problem was that while faxing was almost magical, it required many steps to fax a computer-generated document, such as a letter that you created with Microsoft Word. First you print the document, walk over to the printer, carry the paper to a fax machine (usually in a different room), insert the paper into the fax machine, enter the phone number, wait about 5 minutes for it to send, and then discard the paper. If any of the paper sheets got jammed in your fax machine, or in the customer's fax machine, you had to repeat the entire process. And that happened a lot.

Before computer-fax:
How to send a fax

Before products like "Fax Senior" or "Fax Junior", sending a fax was an error-prone and time-consuming process.

I knew there had to be a better way to send faxes that originated on a computer. There was so much obvious pain: the time wasted doing all of those above tasks just to send a fax, not knowing if the fax you just sent was received properly by the recipient, sending the fax to the wrong number by mistake, no record of when and to whom the faxes were sent, and so on. The pains were numerous and obvious.

I found the pain! Now I had to find the aspirin. That, as it turned out, was actually relatively simple. Using some "off-the-shelf" hardware, we were able to develop technology

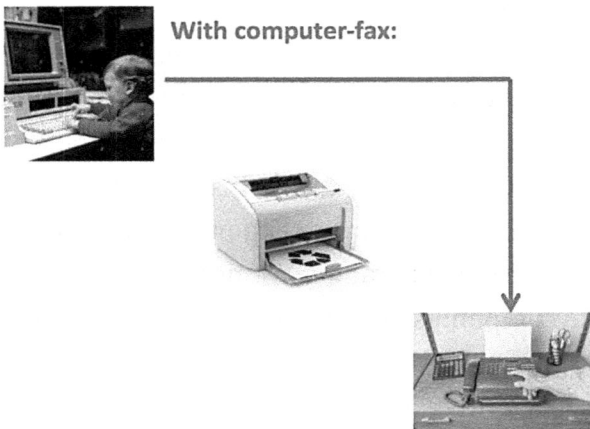

With computer-fax:

With our computerized fax product, the pain was eliminated.

that allowed people to send a fax directly from their computer screen. Here's how it worked: through our system the computer could be connected to a fax transmission device called a "fax modem." Our software sent your document from the computer to the fax modem, and the fax modem would transmit the fax to the recipient's fax machine.

Besides increasing efficiency, this new method massively reduced paper cost and waste. It was streamlining at its finest - using technology to make people's lives easier and help businesses run more smoothly in ways they hadn't anticipated.

As I said, we started to build this software in late 1991. By early 1993 we had twelve people working in the company, some helping to advance the technology, others selling to customers, and still others providing technical assistance. Keep in mind that this company was totally bootstrapped; we weren't about to let anyone dilute this idea or our profits by taking outside investment and thus becoming beholden to them.

There were two issues that we had to contend with when we launched our product. First, we weren't the only ones doing it, and second, most companies didn't believe that our product actually worked. There were a couple of other competitors out there selling their fax software - that also worked with a different, more expensive fax modem - in the $3,000 to $5,000 price range. We needed a way to compete with those companies and make it easy for potential customers to trust us.

To be competitive, we came out with two products. First, we built a low-end product named "Fax Junior" that worked with a $95 fax modem and priced it at just $495. That price included the fax modem, so our "margin" was about $400. Sure, it didn't have all the features of our competitor's product, but for $495 the customer was able to send faxes automatically from their computers.

Our higher-end product was named Fax Senior, and it was priced at $1495 (it included a better fax modem). It was still less than half the price of our competitor's product. It had fewer features than theirs. For most customers, the very low price of Fax Junior was what caught their eye. When a customer was deciding between our two products, their attention was "pulled" up to the more expensive Fax Senior. It was almost as if they had mentally committed to spending $495; now paying an additional $1000 for many more features was an easy decision for them.

After we had hundreds of customers, we asked them what other features they wanted. In other words, we were asking dedicated customers what other "faxing" pains we could solve for them. Once enough of the Fax Senior customers had reported that they needed a certain feature, we built it, and then sold it as an add-on to Fax Senior. For example, many customers wanted to include their business logo on the fax page. We sold them the ability to merge graphical logos with the document text for about $100. Others needed to receive a fax and deliver it to someone's desk automatically. We sold this "receive and deliver" feature for about $500. In total we had about $4,000 of individual add-ons.

Had a customer purchased all of our add-ons, they would have spent more with us than our competitors, but pricing both products cheaply enabled us to get through the door easily. People could get started with us without committing to a huge investment. We were initially successful because we were solving a pain. We became *very* successful because we worked with each and every customer to identify new pains and then solved them.

***

Key takeaways:

- **Truly know your customer's pain before you try to become their aspirin.**

- **Listen to what people want before you begin building your product or service.**

- **You can spot pain (and discover an aspirin) in unlikely places.**

- **Try to find more pains and fix them.**

4

Talking:

Make the Whole World Your Focus Group and Network

When trying to lift a start-up off the ground and into the air, one of the biggest mistakes a young entrepreneur can make - or, for that matter, any individual of any age who wants to successfully turn an idea into a viable business reality - is to fail to listen to their anticipated customer base or to those customers who are already beginning to buy or show interest in their idea, product, or service.

At this early stage, it's essential that you listen with the right *open mindset* so that you intuit their true needs. This in turn will allow you to successfully provide them with positive results. Done correctly - by researching the field and asking the right questions - the entrepreneur can often become more aware of their customer's needs than the customers themselves may be. The new business builder must also be able to synch those needs with the realities of the marketplace.

How will you be able to demonstrate the value of your fledgling company if you don't understand your customers on a basic level? The answer is that you won't. You will belly-flop off the diving board into a pool of confusion, excuses and missed opportunities. The *only* way you will be able to deliver your product or service properly is if you understand your objective on a level that brings the challenges into the light - both those challenges already at hand and the ones that lie ahead. That is always more difficult than it seems and requires the power to listen in a focused way that most people don't easily master. But once you tap into this frequency, it will unlock a previously unimagined world of success.

How *does* one listen properly? It comes down to having a dialogue - and not just between you and your customer, but between what you see as your customer's needs and the realities of the world at large. Be sure of one thing: without directly talking to your customers, and more importantly your universe of *potential* customers, your business will not succeed.

All business ventures begin with an idea, a concept, and a possibility. Beyond that you need to get both subjective and objective feedback, and not just live in your own head. Communication is fundamental to bootstrapping success. Unfortunately, this type of communication isn't as easy as talking to a friend. It's a more advanced and sophisticated way of finding answers. It does take time, effort, and energy, and often entails getting out of your comfort zone. If you master this form of communication, as I discovered for myself time after time, you can then position your business to take off in the most powerful way, even effortlessly, because your "plane" will be on the right runway.

To do this effectively you need the right set of skills, and the mental fortitude to be able to guide other stakeholders in the right direction. Some of these skills require cooperation, while some others may create a bit of friction. *All* of them are necessary to get your business up and running in the best possible way, with the best staying power for soaring to success in the long run.

The stories I relate in this chapter are intended to provide a framework through which you will learn how to really understand what your customers need. Some of the examples from my experience are cautionary and can help you avoid the mistakes I made and was forced to learn from. It's far less painful to laugh at my misadventures than to experience these mistakes in your own company.

The cardinal rule here is to avoid moving ahead in a vacuum. That is of critical importance. The vacuum can take many forms, with all of them equally deadly to bootstrapping success. It can take the form of your own preconceived notions of what a customer wants. It can take the form of your resistance to a necessary pivot - more on pivots in Chapter 8. It can also take the form of you giving up on your idea too quickly or abandoning a promising solution or product which has simply been applied to the wrong problem. Lastly, it can take the form of professional arrogance - a willful blindness to the marketplace - a kind of "I know what's best" mentality that you must avoid. Any of these vacuums have the potential to suck your company's very real potential right down the tubes. Too many promising ventures end up in the sewer due to bad or inadequate communication. I'm here to make sure that doesn't happen to you.

***

Talk to Your Potential Customers Rather Than Make Assumptions

In Chapter 3, I introduced you to the story behind **Softbol**, our software converter company. We made several mistakes:

- We didn't properly identify who had the pain.
- We were dependent on someone else (the reseller) doing something "different" for our business to grow.

- We were fooled by our own perceptions – no one cares how great your product is.

What you, the young entrepreneur, need to glean from this example is that even if you have an idea that seems revolutionary, it won't turn into what you thought it would be without the real communication between you and the people who are going to be using it. Unless you test it out - unless you really talk to enough people to figure out its viability - you should not just jump in and build something. With so many startup concepts you will often discover that while many people MAY say it's a cool idea, that doesn't mean anyone's going to pay for it. Make no mistake: you do NOT have a viable idea for a business until people tell you that they will *pay* for what you have.

***

Talk Until You Stop Hearing Something New

This next lesson is also one I learned while bootstrapping **Softbol**. After our roadblock with the resellers, I knew I had to find a different way to make the company work. I needed to find some large computer manufacturers out of Silicon Valley who could become distributors for me—companies who would first pay me tens of thousands of dollars to get my converter running on their computers, and then purchase many copies of the converter to sell, along with their computers, to the resellers.

I knew I needed to speak to dozens of computer manufacturers, but I didn't know what pitch would work on them. I had some ideas but didn't really know what it would take to get them to spend money with me. I decided I needed to visit a bunch of them and learn how to do this by *doing* it. I There were a slew of computer manufacturers in California, so I planned a month-long road trip (I brought along my bicycle) where I would speak to lots of these companies.

I started in San Diego, meeting with computer makers, and at the same time had a ton of fun riding my bicycle up and down the coast. Before I left Boston, I scheduled appointments for each afternoon so I could do my riding in the morning. My plan was this: I would walk in there, tell them what we had, and explain the market and the opportunity. I would go meet with the right people and make my pitch. I knew that, inevitably, I would get my pitch 100% wrong the first time, but that there would be some things they might've liked. I'd take what I learned there and move to another guy up the street and, knowing what didn't work, try a modified pitch the next day.

Keep in mind that this plan was put in place before I had expended a lot of effort into pivoting the business towards computer makers. I was first finding out whether or not they were going to be into it. The only way I could find out if they were going to be into it was by *trying.* I did that day in and day out as I worked my way up the coast on my trusty bike. First San Diego, then up to Los Angeles, then up to Santa Barbara, then Santa Cruz, until I finally got to Silicon Valley. By then, I had probably talked to fifteen or twenty of these companies. Each time I talked to them, I got better and better at figuring out how they thought, what was important to them, and how a deal might be structured.

I spent the entire trip visiting, pitching, trying and learning - and biking. Since I was still collecting information, I didn't want to hit any of the really big players. By talking to the smaller computer makers, I was able to determine what things worked without wasting a pitch meeting on a "big fish" since I would only get one chance with them.

Persistence was important here. You can't just do a focus group one or two times and expect that the feedback is going to be consistent. You need to talk to *tons* of people. You have to keep talking to people until you stop hearing something new. As you begin to hear the same thing repeated enough times from potential customers, you're going to start to say: "Okay, this feedback is something I can trust."

Ultimately, I ended up having to educate the computer manufacturers about the size of the market, the size of the opportunity, how easy it would be for them and how it was a financial decision they could get behind. This bicycle trip through California made me realize that there was a path forward for **Softbol**. Once I got back to my company in Boston from the West Coast, we implemented what I had learned by turning it into action. Having talked to enough companies out there, avoiding the very largest, I was able to get a good feeling for what would work.

Sitting down with my business partner Mark, I said: "Okay, this is kind of what we learned. This is how these computer manufacturers think. Now that we got our act together, let's go after the biggest guy out there." So, Mark and I flew out to Silicon Valley and met with the VP of Sales and Marketing at Altos Computer. Sure enough, right after that we got our largest ever deal - about $50,000 - which was a lot of money back then. We would never have closed that deal if we hadn't literally hit the pavement and found out exactly what we needed to know from dozens of computer manufacturers.

***

Make Sure You're Collecting the Right Information, Not Just What You Want to Hear

As an entrepreneur, one thing you don't want to do is to confine or restrict your company to a narrow idea of who your customer is. If you do that you may well end up missing the point of your business entirely. That erroneous and mis-informed mindset may cause you to miss out on who *really* needs your product. Often, as I discovered for myself, your preconceived "ideal customer" isn't who you should be going after. When you do a focus group, be sure you are talking to the right people and be aware of the potential dangers of collecting bad data. Who you talk to and the methods you use for extracting information from them are vital aspects of focus-grouping.

I'll relate a story about a company I bootstrapped, which almost didn't make it because we failed to properly collect information from the outset. Back in the early 2000's, instant messaging was all the rage. As much as people were using it for fun, companies were also using it for business. If you don't know what instant messaging is, think of it like texting - but between computers instead of mobile phones. As much as we are all hooked on texting now, back then everyone was equally hooked on instant messaging.

Sales people were sending invoices and making commit-ments over instant messaging, but unlike email there was no computer trail. Once the message was sent all evidence is gone. That's not good for a business and that's the pain. We thought - let's create a computer trail for instant messages – that's the aspirin.

We actually stumbled into this business because our

Omtool company encountered this very problem. One of **Omtool's** sales reps made a promise to a customer over instant messaging. No one at **Omtool** – not their manager, nor the Sales VP nor the CFO, knew about the sales rep's deception. That caused innumerable problems for our publicly traded company. If we had that problem, just imagine how many other companies were facing the same issue.

Tens of thousands of companies would need our product, since their employees are sending instant messages all day long. Our product would solve so many "pains" that instant messaging has caused: workplace bullying, sexual harassment, fraud. We were going to be wildly successful.

For market research, I talked to dozens of executives to see if this would be something they would value. I got back a great deal of positive feedback from many of them. There were two other venture capital-backed companies doing the same thing, but their product cost more than three times what our product was going to be sold for. We figured if we offered a much cheaper product, we should be far more successful than those companies were.

We thought we did everything right because:

1. We identified the pain.
2. Customers told us they needed it.
3. We priced it low enough that all companies could afford it.

We named the company **IMbrella**. This was a wonderful marketing name at the time since everyone was using the abbreviation "IM" for instant messaging. Our logo was a woman holding an umbrella over her head - implying that our product will shield you from the dangers of Instant Messaging.

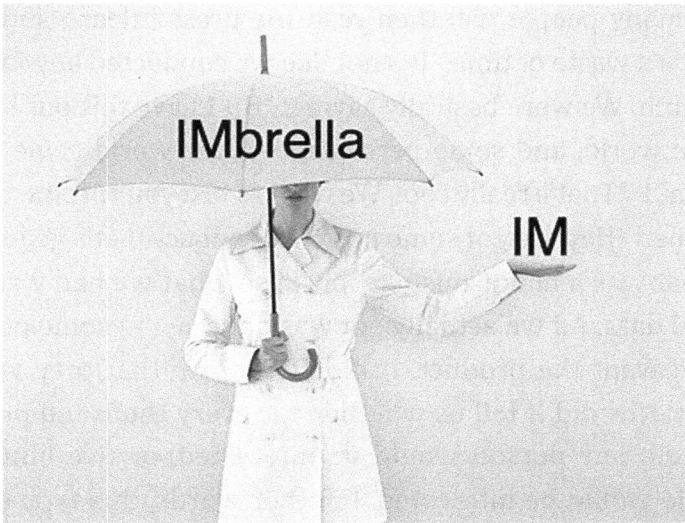

This was the initial imagery used with IMbrella.

To get customers, we started a Google pay-per-click campaign, using keywords like "Instant Message Monitoring" or "IM tracking." We had already talked to a handful of Information Technology (IT) directors to see what phrases they would search for in Google and based our advertisements on those phrases. Several hundred companies contacted us saying they needed something like this, and that they didn't like the fact that competitive products were super expensive. They said they thought our product would be a good fit. Since

We used this imagery in our Google pay-per-click campaign.

we were mainly listening to people who were telling us what we wanted to hear, we thought we had proof of concept and proceeded to try to turn it into a viable product.

When you put out a press release based on positive feedback from those who are telling you your product or business concept is good, you're only hearing one side of the story. You don't know how many people will then read the press release and say: "That's a waste of time." It's not like we conducted any formal research. We were basically saying: "Hi! I have this out here!" to the world, and some percentage of the world came back and said: "That's really cool. We want to test your product." We assumed "Hey, we got some positive feedback. Let's go for it."

That was a major mistake, because what we had was not useful data. All we actually got was data saying some people *would* want the product. It didn't confirm that they would buy it. Nor did it tell us whether, for every thousand people you tell, one person would be interested, or five hundred people would be interested. In other words, this type of information-gathering didn't give us any gauge on how popular this product would be. You can only have that after talking to a lot of people who may not really care about what you've done. All we had to go on was positive feedback. We weren't getting negative feedback because all the negative feedback people didn't click on the ads or contact us.

In retrospect - hindsight always being 20/20 - what we should have done was found the names of about a hundred IT directors of companies, those with annual revenues of between five million and sixteen million dollars a year, in the Boston area where we happened to be living, and set up a focus group. We could have given them pizza and beer for their time - during which we could have asked them a few questions and used that to judge whether or not our **IMbrella** product would be useful enough that they would want to buy it. They probably would have also liked the opportunity to network with other IT managers and given us a couple of hours of their time after work. We didn't even take the simplest step, which would have been to talk to just *ten* of the IT managers at companies that could afford to buy this technology.

As I mentioned earlier, I did talk to executives at dozens of companies and received positive feedback; however, I failed to talk to the principal decision-maker for a product like this. I should have asked IT managers how much money, if any, they would spend to buy this technology.

We launched the **IMbrella** product and – surprise, surprise – it didn't take off. It failed because while most companies did think it was a good idea, it still was not something they were willing to spend money on. I call this a classic fire-extinguisher problem. People only value fire extinguishers after they've had a fire. Before that, they don't really care. With our product, unless a business had a problem that required a computer trail, no one cared.

The lesson here is that if you don't do enough market research and your due diligence by talking to enough people to find out if they really will spend money on your product, you are doing nothing more than hoping for the best. And in business "just hoping" will not get you anywhere except possibly *out* of business. The smart solution: always do your research. Always go down every conceivable avenue of potential customers. You don't want to end up kicking yourself for missing what was right in front of your face.

For the young entrepreneur, the key takeaway from this story is that you need to be aware of a group or a community's needs and desires on a very deep level. Finding a potential audience isn't enough to justify starting a company. If you properly listen to what your customer base is asking for, the community that forms will do much of the tedious groundwork. You won't have to work hard to sell them on it. Where there is a true *need*, and you can fulfill that need, your satisfied customers will do your marketing for you by spreading the word.

***

Don't Allow Your Ego to Overshadow Reality

Inevitably your business will change over time - as it should. This can be a good thing. My note of caution here, because I've seen it happen too often with start-ups, is this: try to not become too attached to an idea just because you were the one who thought of it. Separate your ego from your idea. That's a hard concept for people to grasp, especially when their idea is met with positive reinforcement from people who are kind, but perhaps also not familiar with the challenges an entrepreneur faces in the ever-changing business, cultural, and social landscape.

Friends and family may tell you how wonderful your idea is, and because those people are important to your sense of self, their praise, by inflating your ego, may actually damage your objectivity. Suddenly *you* are great because somebody told you your *idea* was great. But ask yourself these questions:

- Is that person a potential customer?
- If he or she were a stranger, or someone you hoped would invest, would he or she have the same reaction?
- *Who or what are these encouragers really invested in - a realistic concept of my company's potential in the highly competitive marketplace, or their concept of and concern for me?*

Please do not fall so deeply in love with your business concept that you can't handle criticism or even rejection. Those two things are a given. They *will* happen. It's how you react that matters, how you transform your "caterpillar" of an idea into a business "butterfly" of success. Sometimes that initial idea is just the first step in building a business and not what the business will ultimately evolve into.

The best attitude and strategy here is to remain faithful to your own beliefs while also being self-critical. If someone rips apart your idea, don't become defensive: *listen!* If you can't accept that you may be wrong, you are probably on the wrong path. Until you start getting feedback that shows you that you are on the right path, you really have no solid ground to stand on, except faith. Entrepreneurs don't survive on faith - we need to rely on more tangible metrics. If you do that, you'll never end up wondering *why* you failed: you'll know in precise terms what you did wrong. With that knowledge you will be able to regroup or restart.

Some of my ventures have failed, though I don't like the terms "fail" or "failure" and will go into my reasons in the next chapter. Yes, I have made significant mistakes, and gone down many dead-end roads. I have also massively succeeded. That's because no idea was ever too precious to me to change or replace just because I thought it up. The feedback you get isn't the problem: it's the solution. You just have to keep talking to people, asking the right questions, and learning how to listen properly. The flattering encouragement or praise you may have gotten from some people may be false or misleading, and will not serve you well. Once you activate your ability to listen objectively—taking your ego out of the equation—you'll hear what's truly valuable in every observation or criticism.

The bottom line is that your company isn't about you; it's about your customers. They hold the key to your success.

They don't particularly care about you; rather, they care about what you can provide for them. If you can provide them with something that they can't get from anywhere or anyone else, they will change your life. Listen to them in a new way. Get the feedback, as harsh as it might be. Filter it through your own research, observations and innate creative intelligence. Your breakthrough may be just a few "informal focus group" conversations ahead!

***

Key Takeaways:

- **Know your customers better than they know themselves.**

- **Intuit what your customers need, not what you think they want.**

- **Never assume anything about your customers. Always focus-group them first.**

- **Talk to more people than you think you need to. Keep talking until you stop hearing anything new.**

- **Make sure the data you're looking at is actually informative.**

- **Talk to the right people - friends and family aren't focus groups.**

5

Stumble. Fall. Get Up. Do it Again.

A New Take on 'Failure'

Failure, in the dictionary, is defined as a "lack of success" or "the omission of expected or required action." That concept is hammered into our brains early on. In terms of bootstrapping a business, I define failure very differently. To me, learning to re-conceptualize "a lack of success" so that it becomes an unexpected yet powerful learning tool, and then applying that attitude to your day-to-day operations, is an important element in the potential survival of your young venture. It will positively impact your future as an entrepreneur. In other words, seeing missteps as educational rather than discouraging gives you access to the underlying insights behind what you might initially perceive as blunders. This will allow you to learn from every challenge.

There's a common expression in Silicon Valley: *Fail fast.* I prefer to express it as: *Understand why you are failing and fix it.* Sometimes fixing a problem means you need to change your mindset. Other times, it requires bringing in new people with fresh outlooks. And yes, sometimes it does mean cutting your losses and moving on.

If you have to move on from an idea or a start-up, you do not need to walk away empty-handed. By absorbing the information you gained from this experience, you can apply it to your next venture and avoid making the same mistakes. Albert Einstein famously said: "The definition of insanity is doing the same thing repeatedly and expecting different results." Einstein was talking about theoretical physics, but his impeccable logic translates perfectly to the business world. And beyond simply learning from what didn't work - you must learn *better* from your mistakes than other people learn from theirs. Don't fail faster, fail *better*. Fail *smarter*. Fail with courage, and hopefully - with wisdom.

Does this sound contradictory, even impossible to you right now? If so, I'm not surprised. Most people feel the same, seeing a business failure as something to be feared rather than learned from. Several decades as an entrepreneur have disavowed me of that notion. In time, your point of view will also change, and hopefully this chapter will help accelerate that process. I too have failed, and I learned to fail better. In so doing I have succeeded beyond my expectations, was fortunate to make a darn good living along the way, and had a lot of fun in the process.

In this chapter - and throughout the book - I will be candid about my missteps, openly revealing what didn't work for me in a number of my start-up ventures. I have no hesitation showing this to you because I've always believed in myself - always believed I can continue learning. My hope is that you will absorb my stories in a way that benefits *your* business career, *your* life, and *your* attitude as captain of a ship sailing on what can often become extremely turbulent waters.

I have talked about faith before, in a negative way - but only because hope *alone,* without putting in the hard work, is foolish and nets you nothing. At the same time, having hope is important to me and a part of the way I approach startups. When I begin a venture, I don't *expect* it to succeed; I just *hope* it will. I'm eternally positive until it's hopeless. Make no mistake: some ideas *are* hopeless from the outset. It's essential that you temper your enthusiasm and optimism with a keen eye for early indicators of hopelessness. Identifying those "early indicators" of a roadblock or dead-end road ahead is essential, because you need to be realistic about your prospects. Watching for those indicators and not glossing over them will give you a forewarning that your idea is flawed and that your business is in danger.

If that happens, there may still be hope! Not all challenges are deadly. No matter how smart, savvy or enterprising you are, flaws will exist in your thinking, your business model, and, ultimately, your business' monetization. Identifying those flaws, learning from them, and fixing the flaws if you can, or applying that knowledge to new business venture concepts and models, is the only way to move beyond them.

I can assure you that once you create a mindset where you are willing to redefine failure as opportunity, there is no limit to your future success.

***

Fully Commit, Or Don't Invest in The First Place

There are countless reasons why an idea or startup can fail to take off. The point of this chapter is to help you understand *why* and *how* projects do not fulfill your expectations. These are two critically different concepts. The *why* pertains to the reasoning behind a project, while the *how* pertains to the implementation - and incidentally, if the *why* isn't there, the *how* will never follow.

At the outset of a project, you need to be totally sure of your *why* - fully committed to your concept and fully vested in the project. If you, as founder or CEO of a company, are not one-hundred percent on board, why would anyone else jump on your ship? I tell this to fledgling entrepreneurs all the time: you will not succeed unless you are truly dedicated.

Dedication requires a wide range of commitment: your own financial investment, personal grit and, most crucially, all of your energy. Energy - time plus mental fortitude - is the most vital element. Simply put, as the force behind a project you need to be totally invested in it or it won't work.

Of course, it doesn't stop with you. You are the leader, and thus the driving force, but you must make sure your partner or partners, your entire team - if you have one, are also one-hundred percent behind your project. Everyone needs to be on the same page in believing this idea will generate success, capital, and fulfillment. If you, as the team leader, don't inspire confidence, who will?

Let me show you a few potent examples of "failures" in my career that might have been successful had I not committed some crucial bootstrapping sins.

***

Know When to Walk Away

In 2016, Dave Spector, a business associate and friend, came to me with an interesting proposition. His uncle Larry, a professor at the City College of New York, had created a website that taught basic math - from numbers and arithmetic all the way up through calculus. He called it **The Math Page**. From 2000 to 2015, tens of thousands of kids visited his site because it clearly explained concepts to them in ways they were not being taught in class. Given that **The Math Page** had millions of hits a year from students all over the United States, I agreed with Dave that this presented a viable market for us as a great opportunity for launching a business. Our thoughts:

- The demand for mobile apps was exploding. We could convert **The Math Page** into a mobile app.
- Kids prefer using their mobile phones (which are "cool") instead of big boxy personal computers (that their parents use) – the "pain." Providing **The Math Page** as a mobile app would be the "aspirin."
- We already had an existing base of customers: the tens of thousands of students who were using **The Math Page** website and would want the convenience of accessing it from their mobile phone.
- We could start with math curriculum and expand from there. We thought if Professor Larry had math lessons, we could find other professors with curriculums for science, history, English and so on, and cross-market to the same students.

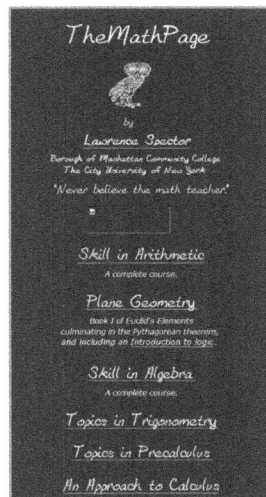

Main screen of **The Math Page** *iPhone app.*

I created a workable app and moved all of Professor Larry's web-based lessons onto both iPhone and Android devices. At launch, we charged three dollars. It was successful for a while because it was "cool" and "convenient." Why use your parent's computer, when, for the price of a Coke, you can get everything you need on your phone?

The giant wall we ran up against was Khan Academy. You may be familiar with Khan Academy because they are still active today. Although, like everything else, their business model has changed somewhat, it was then and still is completely free for students and teachers. Back then they made great educational apps and websites on every subject you can think of. Salman Khan, the man who started it, a highly respected educator and mathematician, simply wanted to educate students worldwide. His product was not just free - it was great.

You can compete with a great product by making yours even better, and then out-market the competitor. You can also compete with a free product that isn't great. But it's very hard to compete with a great free product.

Could we have taken our product in a direction that could also be great and free? Perhaps, through an advertising-sponsored model. But the real failure for this business was that we were not sufficiently dedicated in our business to fight this battle, whereas Salman Khan was. If you are going to invest your time into something, you must commit to be the best in your field. Anything else will be short-lived and doomed to failure.

Our app would have made sense when we did it if Kahn Academy hadn't been there, and we did not recognize this soon enough, so enamored were we with our app concept. While our app *was* generating money and was profitable for a few years, we knew reinvestment was not the right path: we did not have the dedication needed to win. The right option in this case was to walk away. So that's what we did.

***

Pay Attention to Early Adopters and Key Indicators

Every idea, good or bad, has a starting point. It's that moment when everyone involved is ecstatic and energized. Every idea also has an endpoint: that moment everyone involved is either making money or has become fundamentally disappointed. Most often, a flawed starting point will lead to a dismaying outcome. And as entrepreneurs we aren't in the business of dismaying outcomes.

As an entrepreneur, you need to know whether or not your business is viable *before* you invest your time and energy. No matter how convinced you are of the genius of your concept, you need to investigate your market and see what the hard data has to say about your prospects.

As you might have guessed, my mind is always actively thinking of new ventures. Let's examine an unlikely business idea, one that might surprise you, because it involves *salsa dancing.* To surprise my wife Alla, I started taking salsa lessons when we moved to Miami, mainly to better acclimatize to the Latin culture; soon she joined the class. After lots of practice - especially on my part - she became an excellent dancer, and I achieved passable competence.

One day, my salsa teacher Oscar, approached me and asked for advice on creating a salsa teaching app, which I gladly gave him. The idea was for Oscar to have an app into which he could upload instructional videos, then sell the app to his existing students so they could practice at home. Right around this time, I had been curious about how to build iPhone apps, and this idea gave me the encouragement to learn more about how to program an app. In fact, this was a good way to learn iPhone app development. It never hurts to pick up more skills in life.

Anyway, once I completed the app for Oscar, I wondered if other salsa teachers might have the same need and interest, so I started thinking about how to create a generic version of the salsa app. With it, I reasoned, any salsa teacher could create their individual "storefront" and sell video lessons to their own students. Oscar had estimated that he would probably sell around two thousand dollars' worth of video lessons to his own students each year. That's a lot of extra income for a small studio, especially back then.

I expected that other salsa teachers would be willing to pay about ten dollars per month for this service. I also thought the idea could be expanded to other markets (in other words, it was "scalable"). Beyond salsa lessons, having a video app to sell to one's students could, I reasoned, appeal to any type of dance studio, martial arts studio, cooking class, or sewing class, etc. I soon came up with a plan for a generic app which I called **Take My Class**. It was designed to allow small businesses to take videos, store them in an app, then sell the app.

After a little bit of googling to determine how many independent teachers and studios existed across the country, I realized I was looking at tens of thousands of prospects. The "Total Addressable Market" could generate several million dollars annually! That was enough to stoke my enthusiasm, and I continued my investigation.

To test the market, I selected 250 random studios from all over the country: salsa, ballet, cooking, kick-boxing, etc. I gathered each studio name, description, owner's name, location, phone number, class listing, class schedule and logo.

The next logical step was to let the studio owner know how to record their content and then how to sell the resulting videos to their students directly. To do that I created a website that showed how any of these apps would look on an iPhone. The illustration was of an iPhone that I programmed in such a way that whichever studio person logged, that studio owner would see their individual logo. There were several menu items, including "About," "Classes," "Schedule," "Location," and "Call Us." Again, I was able to ensure that each iPhone picture would call up the exact studio's information.

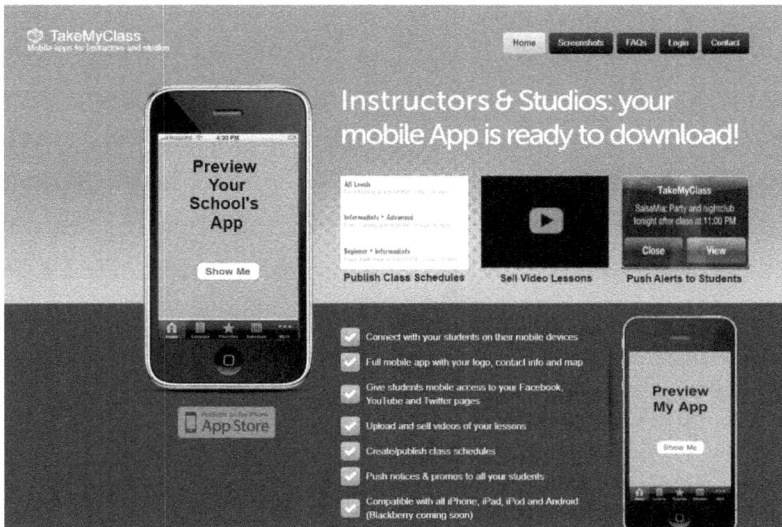

This was the website where each of the 200 studios could view their own "customized" website, to give them the impression that the website and the app were finished.

As a result, each studio owner or teacher who clicked the link in the email we sent them would view a webpage dedicated to their studio at the **Take My Class** website. That studio owner would feel like they were looking at a real app specifically dedicated to their particular studio; which hopefully would motivate them to sign up with us.

Developing this website took me about a month. After that, I sent a compelling email to those two hundred and fifty studios - all different types - offering a thirty-day free trial. Ten percent of the people signed up. That's a very good result: unsolicited emails usually result in a two-percent or lower response. At the same time, I went back to a few teachers I knew personally and told them the app was ready, and that all they had to do was record their videos. Sounds good, right?

There was just one problem. None of those teachers that I knew personally actually went ahead and created any videos. And these were teachers whose businesses were growing year-over-year and who understood the value of marketing. That told me something: if a marketing-conscious studio would not create video lessons, most studios I reached out to online definitely would not create video lessons. If I couldn't get anybody who is super excited about my app to actually *do* something about it, if it wasn't enough of a priority for them, then nobody was ever going to do anything with it. The idea, though great in concept, was not viable in the marketplace!

I knew it was time to let the idea go because these were key indicators telling me I should walk away. Keep in mind that it didn't cost the studios anything to use **Take My Class**; during this test period, for the studios I knew personally, it was free. All they had to do was put in a little bit of time, and they did not. Pay close attention to your early adopters. If the people who say they are excited about what you're doing are not putting forth the effort to actually use it - even before you ask for money - you most likely have a flawed idea.

In this experience I also saw where the future was headed. Free content - in this case, video lessons - was starting to supplant the concept of paid content. YouTube alone changed the world for video lessons. A teacher will no longer try to sell his or her lessons to students. Instead, they post videos on YouTube in order to hopefully attract new customers for their studio.

***

Never Put Your Future In Someone Else's Hands

When bootstrapping a business, never put yourself in a position where the results are based on something working out for you that you cannot control. I did that one time with a business called **CharterHound**. I learned a lot from the experience, and it certainly isn't a model I would ever repeat.

At the time, Dave Spector (my partner from **The Math Page**) and I were interested in developing a new venture where we would be finding customers for an Internet business that would generate significant finder's fees for us. When you have a website that finds a customer for a business, you are paid a finder's fee of about 10% to 15%. For example, if your website "Dentist Finder" lists dentists in town, and someone uses your website to find a dentist, that dentist may pay you 15% of the money he or she makes on the customer's first visit.

To us, *private jet charter travel* seemed like it would be a great entry point into the "finder's fee" business. Hollywood types, rich business people and other high-net-worth individuals all use private jets to go skiing, or travel from Los Angeles to New York for meetings, etc. They usually don't own their own jet; they simply book a private jet to take them and their colleagues from one place to another. This was 2012.

Based on distance, type of jet, and number of passengers, costs could range from $5,000 to $20,000 for either one-way or round-trip domestic travel, so the finder's fee could be in the $500 to $2,000 range or even more.

Another benefit of targeting private jet charters was that this sector was not automated on the web back in the early 2010's. It was ready for "disruption" - i.e. using the Internet to change the playing field. The market was also huge; there are about half a million private jet charter flights per year in the USA.

We had identified the pain – high-net-worth people like saving money just like the rest of us. They insist that their business managers find the best deals, even when hiring a private jet. If their business manager doesn't save them money, they find a new business manager.

There were nearly no competitors for what we were proposing. Private jet charter flights were booked by agents who operate out of their home via telephone. Our plan was to leverage the Internet to get leads, working with a local charter jet broker, who would pay us for those leads and handle all the arrangements. We negotiated with a local charter agent, who agreed to give us half of his commission for each customer we found for him.

Like the other companies we've built, we bootstrapped **CharterHound**. We spent about $10,000 building the website. We modeled it from a combination of Priceline.com, Kayak.com and Hipmunk.com – all flight search companies that are still around today. From the business manager's perspective, our website would find the least expensive jet charter flight that matched their very fussy needs.

The final ingredient was that we needed to be in the top

Get the lowest price onyour next jet charter

Our search technology analyzes hundreds of jet charter sites, databases and brokers to find you the lowest price every time!

Tell us about your trip, we'll start hunting!

* Round Trip ○ One Way ○ Multi-City			
# of Travelers	Type of Aircraft ▼		
From	To		
Depart	Choose CharterHound Departure Date Return		Choose CharterHound Return Date

Multi-city? No problem!

○ Round Trip ○ One Way ○ Multi-City			
# of Travelers	Type of Aircraft ▼		
1 From	To		Choose CharterHound Departure Date
2 From	To	Date	Choose CharterHound Departure Date
3 From	To	Date	Choose CharterHound Departure Date

While this looks like a fairly rudimentary website, it was typical of most travel websites circa 2010. The high-net-worth traveler or business manager could simply pick the dates and itinerary and they were told that our service would hunt down the best price for the jet charter.

three Google postings for private jet charters. That was critical. If we weren't hitting that metric, no customers would see us, and we literally wouldn't get off the ground. Fortunately, we knew a Google expert who knew how to "play" the search engine. He could guarantee your presence on the first page. Based on his success working with some friends of ours, we knew that If we worked with him for six months, **Charter-Hound** would be listed in the first or second spot on Google's search results. For example, if you typed in "jet charter New York LA", **CharterHound** would pop up in the top spot. For those of you who understand the search business, this was SEO (search engine optimization, where you don't have to pay Google for the lead), not PPC (pay-per-click, where Google shows your ad, but when someone clicks on it, they charge you money).

Over the course of six months, using his strategy, we moved from the third *page* all the way to the top listing in Google. As a result, we began to receive inquiries for jet charters, which our local charter agent then fulfilled. We provided the lead; our charter agent did everything else: he found the lowest cost jet charter flight, collected the money, arranged for the high-net-worth customer to be picked up by limo and driven to the regional jet airport, scheduled a pilot, arranged food and drinks for the flight, and had another limo waiting at the destination.

Everything was working as we had planned, and the business began to grow. We then began to reach out to luxury travel companies to ramp the business up further. We were in the process of establishing a partnership with American Express when we hit a snag - one that would ultimately completely derail our business venture.

Google began to realize that a lot of people were using the same algorithmic "tricks" to outfox their search engine. When they realized this, Google completely redid their search engine ranking in a way that relegated us to a back page - a place no business wants to be. Suddenly all the clever tactics we were using had stopped working.

CharterHound's business was built entirely around the expectation that Google's search engine would always work the same way. While we identified this as a risk, we didn't think it would occur anytime soon. We thought there would be enough of a "runway" – time to grow the business – to where Google search rankings would become less critical, and partnerships with luxury brand vendors (such as American Express) would drive most of the business.

In retrospect, that was an absurd hope. At the time it seemed reasonable, since Google hadn't changed its search ranking over the previous five years. I made an assumption that nothing would change quickly. That was our major flaw.

That really bad assumption doomed the business. We had done something I now always warn people about - we had put the success of the company in someone else's hands.

We did try to come up with a variety of alternative marketing strategies to drive the business, but all of them required significant funding and several years to implement. Neither Dave nor I had a personal goal that dictated we wanted to grow a jet charter broker travel business, so we made the decision to abandon the venture.

Our business failed because a key domino – the Google search engine strategy – was in someone else's hands, and that domino fell, taking the business down with it.

When your business is dependent on someone else's actions - actions you cannot control - your business is probably doomed from the outset. At some point that critical domino will fall, and everything you've created will be lost. Analyze every single thing that could go wrong, determine how you will recover, and then decide if the recovery from such an event still makes that business exciting to you. Otherwise, come up with a different strategy or a different business.

***

Pay Attention to the World Around You

At the beginning of 2017, I and Bob Voelk, my partner in two of our most successful companies, decided that we wanted to build another company together. At the same time, we didn't feel like creating another company from scratch. Our thought was that instead of being entrepreneurs, we might become angel investors by forming a new company which we gave the name **Fruition Funding**.

Checking out the marketplace, we found lots of entrepreneurs who had ideas, but wanted way more money than we felt their companies were worth. In fact, every time we found a company worth looking at, the CEO thought it was worth far more than what we calculated. That in itself gave us an idea. We knew how most venture capitalists worked: they would invest in about twenty companies, knowing only one or two of them would be very successful. Our idea was to go to some of these venture capital firms and say: "Tell me about the companies you have that you're ready to shut down or just don't think they will go anywhere. Let **Fruition Funding** buy them from you."

Our concept was to basically recapitalize these companies by first figuring out what the company was doing wrong, re-purpose their technology to help a "niche" of customers, recapitalize the company, and then take the company through the transition. We would probably replace the CEO and run it ourselves for a while as we launched it into a new and probably smaller marketplace.

Bob are I are pretty good at finding a "pain" that could be ameliorated with a technology product, so our idea was to pivot one of these companies to focus on a small niche of customers. After a few years, we would sell this now-profitable company and make sure everyone (staff, original venture capitalists and the customers) would be properly taken care of.

We approached a number of venture capitalists. Not one of them was willing to admit that any of the companies in their "investment portfolio" were "losers," even the ones we could clearly identify as not working. Our showing interest made the VC think that the company *was* valuable. As soon as VCs saw that someone was interested in that company, they decided to figure out how much cash they could get out of us.

This brought us to the conclusion that, since everybody out there seems to think their company is worth way more than it is, we really shouldn't be trying to buy companies. Instead, we should create from scratch - yes - create another company ourselves. Which is what we were experts at anyway!

During the six months we pursued **Fruition Funding**, we had failed to pay enough attention to macroeconomic trends. In the boom economy since 2017 - and especially in the Internet sector - there was too much money chasing too few good deals. It was not a good time to be an investor; it was a great time for all those startup entrepreneurs. In Silicon Valley, for example, entrepreneurs were raising millions of dollars for really silly ideas. In our opinion, none of these companies would ever become viable, profitable or salable.

At **Fruition Funding**, we analyzed so many companies that we were in a good position to recognize how difficult it is to be an angel investor or venture capitalist. Most of the companies you see are fraught with risk: their potential market size is small, their management team is inexperienced, they don't understand the customer's pain, and they haven't proven that if they did receive an investment, they could scale the business. We decided that if we did create a new business we would eliminate as many risks as possible for potential investors.

***

Key Takeaways:

- **Fully commit, or don't invest your time or resources in the first place.**

- **Look out for early adopters. If the people who are most excited about what you're doing are not putting forth the effort to actually use it even before you ask for money, you probably have a flawed idea.**

- **Don't put the future of your company in someone else's hands. You cannot count on them doing something (or continuing to do something) that will enable your business to prosper.**

- **Determine what dominos will doom your business and determine how you will react to those dominos falling.**

- **Pay attention to the world around you.**

- **Do a post-mortem of your failure: determine what you did wrong, and what actions you should take in the future.**

- **Once you redefine failure as opportunities, there is no limit to your future success.**

6

Mentor Connect:

Why You Need Them and They Need You

In the business of being their own boss, most entrepreneurs are independent-minded, strong-willed, and resistant to authority figures they believe are limiting their creativity. This mindset, while an important **aspect of the entrepreneur's** identity, should always be tempered by an ability to listen to and learn from veterans of the game.

Connecting with mentors is an essential part of a young person's professional development - in fact every entrepreneur needs at least one. Consider this for yourself. The right mentor can help you avoid common pitfalls, teach you problem-solving techniques, and, most crucially, give you a set of cognitive tools that allows you to move effectively in a myriad of challenging situations that you may well find yourself facing.

Finding and developing a productive relationship with a mentor requires strong communication skills, plenty of persistence, and an ability to alter long-held assumptions. It's not as simple as emailing the CEO of your favorite company to ask him or her for advice. In seeking out a mentor, be aware of exactly what you want from the situation - and also what *you* bring to the table. Make sure this mentor is the right one for you, or else you'll only waste your time, and theirs. Know also that mentors aren't magic cure-alls who will suddenly open doors for **you or invest millions of dollars in your company. At** the same time, successful people - especially highly successful people - do want to give back. Approach every interaction as an opportunity and keep an open mind while maintaining a critical eye toward the situation.

This chapter will help you navigate this complex process of obtaining and working with a mentor, which can be as challenging as it can be rewarding. I will help you understand exactly what functions a mentor serves, show you methods that will help you connect with mentors, provide insight into how the minds of mentors work, and illustrate my ideas with examples from my own career. Think of me as your mentor for finding a mentor.

Part I: What Purpose Does A Mentor Serve?

The main function of a mentor is to give insightful feedback in a way that encourages independent thought in the mentee. Ideally, they offer new ways to look at and analyze a problem and show you that the approaches you are taking or plan to take are not all the possible approaches. A good mentor will tell you what won't work in a way that allows you to identify these issues for yourself when they arise again in the future.

Mentors give young entrepreneurs the perspective needed to understand the highly competitive world they are about to enter. These seasoned professionals have a birds-eye view of the world, while people just starting out often can't see the forest for the trees. An experienced mentor will have enough life experience to know when you are going down the wrong path and can give advice on how to expand your viewpoint to solve the problems you are encountering or may soon encounter. Seasoned entrepreneurs understand that all business problems have common issues, whether yours is a big or small business. Experience gives them the ability to predict with great accuracy what might happen and show you ways to optimize each situation.

Contrary to popular belief, a mentor's most valuable asset is not the ability to open doors or introduce you to powerful connections. Those things can happen, but you should view them as an added bonus. What you *should* expect from a mentor is an ability to show you how to look at problems in a different way, opening up new "thought-pathways." This will allow you to glimpse into the mindset that got him or her to where they are so you can apply that mindset to your situation. Soon enough you will learn how to go down those thought-pathways by yourself.

A good mentor will ask leading questions that will cause you to think about new ways to attack a business problem. Sometimes a mentor will play devil's advocate, pushing the right buttons to lead the mentee towards the best conclusion. A mentor will keep asking more questions, not unlike a psychologist would do with a patient. This includes: "What are you trying to accomplish?" "Why and how do you think you can get there?" A mentor will first and foremost help an entrepreneur focus on his or her personal goals, because if you don't know what your personal goals are, you're never going to get anywhere, since all the decisions will be arbitrary. With a set of personal goals, you will build your business around fulfillment of those pre-set goals.

Say, for example, that you are trying to start a company which provides artisanal beans to coffee houses at low prices and feel you need a mobile app that will allow coffee shop owners to view your supply options and order from you directly. When you contact software developers, they say it will cost fifty thousand dollars to build out the technology. It's money that you simply don't have. Forward progress is stalled, and frustration sets in.

At this point, let's further imagine that you go to your mentor and say: *I can't do anything until I come up with fifty thousand dollars.* An adroit mentor would ask you these questions:

- *Do you really need that app? Is that app going to solve your problem, or is your problem that you don't have enough face time with the buyers from these coffee shops?*
- *Do other suppliers they are doing business with have apps?*
- *Have you gone to any of the coffee conventions where buyers convene?*
- *Have you played the role of being a coffee shop owner and talked to your potential competitors?*

A mentor can help you understand that even if you had this app, it doesn't mean people are going to start buying from you. They could show you that you need to collect data in an ever-widening circle until you see a clear path to success. If you consider the problem correctly, you may discover, in this example, that the problem was not ease of access but rather that your beans are not unique enough, or that they fail to meet fair-trade standards that are currently in vogue.

In the end, you may find that the problem you thought you would be solving with the app wasn't the real problem. You might have discovered that coffee shop owners were generally happy with their suppliers but fed up with finicky expensive roasting machines that are always breaking down. You might then go back, re-examine your personal goals, and realize that your true goal is to help coffee houses, but not in the importing of trendy beans. Suddenly you're in the business of being a coffee *roaster*, one who can drop-ship roasted beans to coffee houses all over the country - and you didn't waste fifty-thousand dollars on a useless app!

In this hypothetical example, a mentor forced you to go back and ask the kinds of questions that led you to realize that you had picked the wrong problem to solve. Had you not worked through this with your mentor you would have failed to understand the real pain that needed alleviation. Mentors can help you decipher what is pertinent information that moves you towards the goal rather than random information that moves you further away.

Mentors Can Come in Unlikely Packages

My first mentor was atypical in more ways than one. His name was Dick Berthold, and he was one of the partners at Cortex, a Boston software company where I worked summers while in college. Back then I rented a room in an MIT frat house and spent all my time working on computers, solving problems, and trying to learn as much as possible. This was heaven for a kid like me!

I reported directly to Dick, which was much easier said than done: Dick had a unique conversation style, to say the least. He was in his late thirties and had zero social skills, but he was probably a genius working with computers. I knew I could learn from him, no matter how challenging he made the process.

We had developed a routine. Dick would give me a problem; I would go back and ask if he wanted me to do it this way or that way in implementing the programming. In response, Dick would grunt. You read that right. Grunting was his primary method of communication with me. Sometimes we would have an actual conversation during which he would ask me why I had done something a certain way, but grunting was much more common, and clearly much preferred by Dick. Essentially, Dick would give me no information or direction whatsoever. By providing only a positive grunt when I was on the right path and a negative grunt when I was on the wrong path, he left me on my own to solve problems.

Fact is, he was actually saying a lot with those grunts. He knew I could solve most problems he threw at me, so he was saying (grunting) that I should solve it in any way I wanted, as long as I creatively came up with the right solution. Over time, I came to understand that if I was going to build something, I was pretty much on my own, that no one is going to tell me how to figure it out. Thanks to Dick, I learned a lot about how to survive and be responsible for my own actions in the workplace. It was an unusual situation to go through at such a young age, but a good one, as it taught me to be very self-sufficient. That notion was reinforced when I started my first company. I was glad Dick had trained me to be so independent, and to always, first and foremost, think for myself. And no, in case you're wondering, I did *not* become a grunter myself.

Learn How to Think Deeper

Thankfully, the rest of my mentors actually spoke. Perhaps my most important mentor after Dick was a man named Sherm Uchill. I originally met Sherm when he was also at Cortex, as the CEO. I always liked him because he thought differently and wasn't at all corporate. He was like a father figure. I was twenty-five and he was in his fifties when we re-connected. He turned out to be someone who taught me how to *dissect a problem into its components and dependencies and solve each of its components.* If your mentor can provide this to you, you've struck gold.

When my partner Mark and I started **Softbol**, we went to Sherm, who had left Cortex and was running an independent Apple computer store in downtown Boston. It was called **Sherman Howe**. He used that name because people who had just bought an Apple computer would come into the store and say: "*Sherman, how* do I do this?" He did have a great sense of humor and was also extremely forward-thinking. This was the time of the Apple II and Sherm saw the power of putting computers in the home. He actually recognized, as far back as 1981, how much this was going to revolutionize the world.

We asked Sherm to be an advisor to us on the **Softbol** project. Thankfully, he was excited about it. I was confident that Sherm would jump at the idea, since he was always try-ing to push boundaries, and loved becoming involved with exciting new projects. We developed a sort of routine: Sherm met with Mark and I monthly for lunch at the restaurant in the same building as his store. Over lunch we'd give him a rundown of what we were up to. If we reported a problem, he would tell us to come up with all our possible solutions, including evaluating the upsides and downsides of each, and then present all of this to him. At the end of lunch, when the bill came, Sherm would pull out his AMEX card. That restau-rant didn't take AMEX – I assume Sherm knew that since he always ate there - so Mark and I were forced to pick up the bill. This, in retrospect, was fine – we, after all, were getting free advice.

I always tell people that if you can't convince your mentor that a plan is great, you had better come up with a different plan. In our monthly meetings, Sherm would play devil's advocate, asking us to consider every possible hurdle that could be thrown our way. "But what if *this [insert terrifying business problem here]* happens," he would always say. He was making sure we analyzed where we were going - to a dizzying degree. Sherm always pushed us to dive another level down to where the real treasure was buried - to think deeper.

There came a time when Mark and I were trying to close a deal for **Softbol** with Altos, a now-defunct computer manufacturer in Silicon Valley. Their business model was similar to the way all computer companies operated from the 1960's through to the 1990's - they manufactured computers and sold them through a network of regional computer resellers.

These computer resellers wrote their own accounting or time-keeping software - usually for doctors, dentists, lawyers or restaurants - in a computer language that only worked on that manufacturer's computer. In previous chapters I talked about **Softbol**, the converter that Mark and I created. As I explained, that converter enabled any reseller who had created software written in a computer language that was "locked" on computers made by Digital Equipment Corporation (DEC), to be usable on all of the new microcomputers coming out of Silicon Valley. One such microcomputer manufacturer in Silicon Valley was Altos Computer.

We pitched Altos on the idea that they could make direct use of the thousands of resellers who normally sold DEC computers by convincing them to sell Altos computers, using our **Softbol** converter. Given that the Altos computers sold for one-tenth the price of a similarly powered DEC computer that would be a win for Altos, a win for the reseller, and a win for us.

Mark and I had been talking to a Vice President at Altos for about two months. We had finally gotten to the point where we were going to be flying out to Silicon Valley to close the deal. This was a big opportunity, but frankly we didn't know how to handle this negotiation. At that point, we were basically two programmers in a garage with no idea of how the business world worked. In truth, we didn't know what we were doing.

A few weeks before our meeting we went to Sherm. He made us map out an entire list of possibilities and go through every possible scenario on how this meeting could go. Mark and I stayed up all night drawing up a logic tree that was ten or twelve items deep. It had every question the Altos VP might ask, and questions we meant to ask him. We put it up on the wall, working from box to box through every conceivable possibility, Question and Response, Question and Response. Finally, we were sure we knew what to say to get to the point where we would close a contract.

When we showed our chart to Sherm, he implored us to look at even more questions - to dive a few levels *deeper.* We did that, again pouring over every possible scenario. It was mentally demanding work, but it paid off. Our company, **Softbol**, closed a fifty-thousand-dollar contract with Altos, which in today's dollars would be more like one-hundred and fifty thousand dollars. If Sherm hadn't been there to advise us and push us to not be satisfied until we had mapped out scenario after scenario, I don't think we would have been well enough prepared for that meeting. We might have looked like the innocents we actually were. Instead, we closed the first major deal for our company.

Sherm hadn't given us the answers: he had forced us to come up with them ourselves. He taught me to question every one of my decisions until I got to the heart of the matter. I'm still applying that process to my business practices today.

Mentors Help You Access the Necessary Pieces Needed to Grow Your Business

Sherm also assisted Mark and me in finding some key players to help us get **Softbol** off the ground in its early stages. Long before we ever got close to closing that Altos deal, Sherm helped us make sure that we had a proper foundation in place so that we didn't get off to a rocky start. One thing we needed was a good lawyer who could incorporate the company. Because Sherm was so well-connected, he was able to get us a meeting with one of the top attorneys in Boston. We met Sherm at Hale and Dore, an old school white-glove law firm that serviced the highest tech companies in New England. Sherm told us that this particular lawyer was on the board of the Boston Symphony, was on the boards of many of the largest corporations in New England and was on a first-name-basis with the Governor and the Mayor. To say this man was outside our circle would be a massive understatement.

Mark, Sherm and I got off the elevator on the forty-fifth floor and walked down a long hallway, trodding lightly on an elegant and plush two-inch carpet. The lawyer's office was the size of a large apartment. When we opened the doors, there he sat, intimidatingly, behind a massive desk on the far side of the room with only two chairs in front of him. Sherm pushed Mark and I forward. We sat down like two school kids in the principal's office.

He took a long look at us. We were wearing jeans and button-down shirts. He was wearing what looked like a three-thousand-dollar suit. After the inspection he turned and focused his glance directly at me.

"How old are you?" he asked, without any pleasantries.

"Twenty-eight," I replied.

He let out a low-rumbling laugh and said: "You'll make it." Sherm had clearly given us a vote of confidence, and with him that carried weight. As it turned out, this lawyer not only helped incorporate our company - for a small amount of stock in lieu of a fee we would have never been able to afford - he also ended up acting as a legal mentor. I didn't want to take up a lot of his time and frankly I *was* intimidated by him, but if we were about to sign a contract with a major Silicon Valley manufacturer, I would shoot it over to him. He would have one of his associates look it over and send it back with corrections. Knowing you have that kind of lawyer behind you makes you feel much more comfortable as a young, wide-eyed optimist bootstrapping a business. It's always nice to have some firepower on your side so that you won't get taken advantage of.

We also needed to do PR and advertising, but we certainly didn't have the money for those things either. So Sherm introduced us to a publicist named Bob Strayton. Bob was a friend of Sherm's from the Wellesley Golf Club. He said he would help us out, and he did. He set us up with a team of two of his PR people. Mark and I had come up with the name **Softbol**, and Bob's PR company devised a baseball theme for the advertising campaign, which created a brand. They made sure we were in the trade magazines and ran ads for us, which was a crucial step in generating awareness for **Softbol**.

Since Bob was a good friend of Sherm's, he let us run up a pretty stiff tab. When we signed the major deal with Altos, I wrote him a check for the balance. I barely had a salary, but I knew the first thing we had to do was pay the people who had been carrying us for so long. In the end, Bob probably wouldn't have cared whether or not I paid him, but it was the right thing to do. That's an important element of the mentor relationship: always do right by the connections they set you up with. Integrity is paramount. Otherwise, you may end up sabotaging the relationship of trust and respect that you built with your mentor. If you do that, doors stop opening. The last thing I would have ever wanted to do was to disappoint Sherm, and I never did.

Incidentally, this doesn't mean that you have to work with every person a mentor connects you to. As I mentioned earlier, Sherm set us up with a venture capitalist willing to invest quite a bit of money in us. However, there were stipulations with which we were not comfortable, so we politely declined and said we would rather bootstrap. Mentors will often have all types of connections, and whether you want to use them or not depends entirely on your personal goals. Ideally, your mentor should guide you through this process, and not push people on you if you think they are not a perfect fit. So, at **Softbol** we worked with Sherm's lawyer and PR firm but not with one of his venture capitalist friends, and he was pleased we had thought it out enough to make our own informed decision. We capitalized on what made sense for us and left what we didn't think would help our company.

Mark and I got lucky with Sherm's connections, and chances are you will get lucky with your mentor's connections, too. But I never fully relied on them. It was never a make or break because of outside influences. When bootstrapping, you want to make sure you take advantage of each and every opportunity presented or door opened, but do not count on those things happening. With Sherm, the most precious thing he provided, and what you should *absolutely* expect from your mentor, was an education, a critical eye, support, and his ability to show us new and more profound ways to solve problems. Those are the things which are as good as gold.

* * *

Part II: How to Find A Mentor

People often ask me: *How do I find a mentor?* and *What kind of person should I be looking for?* I tell them that they should look for someone between the age of forty to seventy, who has done something similar to what you are trying to achieve. When you contact them, you have to sell them on a) who you are, b) how your idea is significantly interesting, and c) why you are worth their time.

I know it feels intimidating to ask someone, out of the blue, to mentor you. There are some practical things you can do to help alleviate those fears. Attending conferences or business-oriented meet-ups is a good way to meet people in a social setting. Push past your anxiety and introduce yourself to people you find interesting. Do it in a direct but respectful way. Make sure you have your personal and professional elevator pitch down to about forty-five seconds.

Now here's the hard **part: expect** that for every ten people you reach out to, *maybe* one will say yes. You have to learn to be okay with rejection. The good news is that you don't need a large number of successes to make a mentor connection: you just need one good one. If you are going to be an entrepreneur, you have to learn early-on that getting rejected *a lot* is going to be the norm. And that one ***yes*** response could potentially be worth thousands of rejections.

As you engage in this process, you are going to initially mess up. Jumping into something new, it's inevitable you'll do it **wrong. There** is no reason to assume you'll know how to do it right. Accept that difficult truth and move on. You have to keep pushing until you have absorbed the feedback from previous rejections and start to not get rejected. Be attentive, listen to feedback, let people criticize what you are doing. You will learn something from each refusal and can tailor your pitch so that it is consistent with who you are as a person and consistent with where you want to go. Do this over and over again until you are saying something people are eager to respond to.

Connect Emotionally

Once you have slogged your way through the waves of inevitable rejections and learned to refine your pitch, you will start to see some favorable responses. It is an incremental process. You will go from failing 100% of the time to failing 90% of the time, to failing 80% of the time. Eventually, you'll have refined what you're saying enough that it really strikes somebody emotionally. People only do things for emotional reasons. Always remember that when you are pitching someone - under any circumstance. The trick here is to get the *objective* world to care about your *subjective* story.

This concept is especially important when trying to link up with a mentor. You have to convince them that you have what it takes. They need to believe in your drive and your grit. Even the way you carry yourself might favorably influence and entice them. Suddenly they will like what you're saying and will say the magic words: *I get it, and I think I can help you.*

In the beginning try to connect with multiple mentors so you can test out which one is right for you. You will find some great ones who don't want you. You'll find ones that want you but are not a good fit. Keep trying. Trust your gut and expect that some relationships just won't work out.

Offer Something of Value

I was very fortunate to have found Sherm so early in my development, and lucky that he was so willing to take me on as a mentee. Mark and I had brought something to the table in that relationship that we perceived had value: ten percent of the company in exchange for his help. Looking back, I'm sure he knew the stock would never be worth anything – the likelihood of success was minimal. But he saw we were offering something we perceived had value, and that factored into his decision. If you do not come to your potential mentor empty-handed, you will create a feeling of mutual respect. No matter how little you have, the offer will be meaningful to a successful person: they will just be happy you made the generous gesture.

That offer can come in many forms. Say you are a college student and want to forge a relationship with a brilliant marketing professor. Offer to volunteer in their office, or maybe do some administrative work, in exchange for some of their time and advice. If you can do something you are good at for them that doesn't eat up too much of your own time, then you are helping them, and they will likely want to give back to you. A little sincere flattery also doesn't hurt.

Before approaching a mentor, understand where they are coming from. Understand what is important to them. Make sure that if you are going to commit to do something for them that you can and will commit to it one hundred per- cent. Never be lackluster in your attitude. See yourself "all in" with regard to this relationship and enjoying it. You can't fake anything. People will know. Reticence or resentment to- ward a situation that you asked to be in will only sabotage your goals. Know what you are getting yourself into and be not only okay but enthusiastic. That energy will propel a mentor/mentee relationship to great heights.

* * *

Part III: People Want to Give Back, So Don't Be Afraid To Ask

I've talked to many entrepreneurs in their twenties and thirties who are too intimidated to reach out to mentors. They think: *Why would a successful person in their forties, fifties or beyond want to mentor me? I have no shot.*

As someone who has mentored many people, I want to disabuse you of this notion. You *do* have a shot at finding a great mentor because smart successful people *want* to give back. Let me instill in you the confidence of knowing that there are many people in the business world who will want to be your mentor. If you reach out in the right way, you won't be shouting into a deep canyon with only your own echo to answer you. People who have made it don't exist in an echo chamber. They want to make themselves available to smart young people. When you talk to someone, you have to be in love with your idea or venture and be prepared to show them why they should be in love with it, too.

Money Isn't Most Mentors' Motivation

I'll tell you something that might be surprising: most mentors' motivation won't be financial gain. In fact, money has very little to do with why they might want to help you. You might not believe that, but it's true. **Many people** in the upper echelons are concerned with the ideas behind what others are doing and concerned with ways to improve the world and make it a better place now and for future generations. If they see that you have a promising project and can and will keep that vision alive for however long it takes as you go about building this entity, they will most likely want to help you build it.

I know this because I myself enjoy mentoring young people. I *love* helping smart dedicated people with transformative ideas - almost nothing excites me more. I find giving back to be a foundational aspect of why I got into the bootstrapping game. Of **course, the young entrepreneur will have to approach me in the right way, get me excited about the idea, and** make me believe that a potential future collaboration is worth my time. I'll outline some instances of how young entrepreneurs successfully engaged me as examples that you hopefully can apply to *your* efforts.

I met Brett at a small venture capital conference in New York City, where he was networking and testing the waters for an app called Decision Fish. He had built that app to help the average person improve his or her financial literacy. He had his elevator pitch down pat, caught my attention with his focus and energy, and followed up with me very professionally and effectively. Three big wins right off the bat.

What really drew me in was Brett's emotional impact: the excellent reasons behind why he wanted to launch this software. He had grown up with a single mom who had a very tough time while raising him: there was no financial literacy in their household. He knew he wanted to design an app that would help teach people how to take better care of their money. He was very dedicated; that much was evident immediately. When he told me his back story it inspired me to say: *Okay, I get it, there are probably ways I can help you.*

Brett would call me up once a month or so, asking for feedback about his recently past or upcoming meetings with bankers or distributors. I would always try to make time for him. Once I spoke to him for forty-five minutes from my cell phone while I was stuck in traffic in a New York taxi.

At another point Brett sent me a PowerPoint presentation he was hoping to use to win a grant or award from a bank's finance contest. What he had was very business oriented and very dry. My advice to him was to use the same emotional resonance he had when approaching me. I explained to him that within the first two slides you have to grab somebody by the heartstrings and make them understand that what you're doing is important not only to you but also to *them.* I told him to "keep going back to that over and over again in your presentation. Make it an emotional pitch, and not just another business pitch. If you can make it an emotional pitch, you'll grab them!"

It's often said that when you make a pitch people don't remember what you said, they remember how you made them *feel*. Brett took my advice, and even though he did not win that particular grant he has used this approach to powerful effect and already achieved many significant successes.

Offer Something So You Stand Out

I met a young man named Matt when he was working as a life coach for several of my close friends. They raved about his commitment and energy. As I got to know him, I observed those qualities in him firsthand. A few years ago, he came upon an opportunity to become a co-owner of a tennis academy in Delray Beach, Florida. It was one of the best tennis academies in the country. He had always been a tennis coach and being a partner in this tennis academy was a lifelong dream - so much so that he was willing to give up his lucrative life coaching practice and dive into the tennis academy full time.

Matt needed someone to help him out with the business side of things, and he came to me. As much as I liked and respected Matt, I could see that taking on this project of advising him was going to require a massive commitment of my time and energy. But Matt was smart - he bartered with me, leading with what made him unique. He suggested that he could trade being a life coach for a friend or member of my family in exchange for me mentoring him and his two partners in the tennis academy. That worked for me, and soon we were off and running.

In exchange for Matt's excellent life coaching services for someone I cared about, I held a monthly board meeting for him and his partners at the tennis academy. I would go over the financials with them, discuss what their short- and long-term goals were, and what problems they were currently dealing with. For over a year, Matt got to live out his lifelong dream of running an academy, with me as someone watching his back on the business side of things. He had incentivized me in a way that made me not only willing to help but excited about his project.

After a year, Matt realized that running a tennis academy was not what he really wanted, but he had learned so much from running his own business that he was able to go on to bigger and better things. He is now working his dream job with a renowned celebrity entrepreneur, and I appreciate that he credits a lot of his success to the business lessons I instilled in him. I believed in Matt because of his passion for tennis, but also because he let me know he was serious by offering me something in return. As I said before, always try to offer a mentor something of what makes you stand out. It will create a two-way street where everybody wins.

Do Your Research Before Reaching Out

Recently I've been doing some volunteer mentoring as part of Florida Atlantic University's "Tech Runway" formal mentoring program. Programs like these are great ways for you to meet potential mentors because you know these people are ready and willing to dedicate their time.

In this program, I met with one entrepreneur who had developed some software that enables not-for-profit organizations to barter the excess capacity of things they might have. An example of his model would be a not-for-profit that has a kitchen which they only use for two hours a day. Another not-for-profit has a high-end camera. The first non-profit needs the use of such a camera for social media posts; the second company with the camera wants to offer cooking lessons to their clients. Using his app, they can barter, and each get what they need without cash. His thought was that it would create community between organizations and allow for the sharing of resources in a mutually beneficial way.

I liked his idea but had some questions about how deeply he had delved into the problem. I asked: *Have you gone around to all these non-profits and asked them if this is an actual problem that they have?* His answer: *Not really.*

I told him that the first thing I would do if I were in his shoes would be to talk to fifty operations directors and ask them open-ended questions about their day-to-day needs. If he did that, he would learn what problems they were really having. Possibly the problems he thought he would be solving were important to him but weren't as important to them.

The point here is that nobody, not even a mentor, will want to look at your product unless you're addressing a problem that you are certain truly exists. If you don't know the issues you might just have "a solution in search of a problem." That isn't going to excite a mentor, and it certainly isn't going to excite customers. This particular student has yet to do his research and, consequently, I'm not particularly excited about putting my time and energy into helping him unless he gets his head out of the sand and takes a serious look around. Perhaps he will. If so, then at that point I will be glad to help him.

Clearly, you will need to do a good deal of research *before* approaching a mentor. Otherwise, as I keep emphasizing for good reason, you'll be wasting your time and the mentor's. If I had talked to more people when I was starting out, and had I actually figured out what the real problems were, I could have saved myself years of time, money and frustration. I hope my examples will save you this angst and put you on the right path much sooner.

***

Key Takeaways:

- **Mentors serve a purpose: to give insightful feedback in a way that encourages independent thought.**

- **Don't let youthful pride get in the way of finding a good mentor.**

- **Take advantage of offered connections, but expect closed doors. It is, to some extent, a numbers game.**

- **Lead with what makes you unique. Engage people emotionally. People only do things for emotional reasons.**

- **You are going to mess up. You are going to get rejected. Accept this fact and learn from each experience.**

- **Many successful people care about changing the world. They will give back if they see something in you.**

- **Always bring something back to the table, no matter how small.**

7

When to Hire?

After You Learn How to Do It Yourself

There comes a point in every entrepreneur's journey when he or she can no longer go it alone. Hiring employees is a necessary part of building a business, even one that is bootstrapped and on a budget. Onboarding the right team members and letting them know exactly what you need from them is crucial to your company's success. If you master this skill-set, your project's growth has the potential to be exponential. Conversely, if you hire the wrong fit for your needs, the amount of time and money you might waste will be catastrophic.

My core philosophy when it comes to hiring is simple: you need to learn how to do something yourself before you expect someone else to do it. You, as the leader, must be one hundred percent aware of what it will take for someone to meet your benchmark of performance. You need to know that *before* you hire someone.

Even if your potential employee has an impressive background in a field or job function, without proper guidance, they will have no idea of how to help you achieve what you're trying to accomplish. You will gain at least a working knowledge of each position in the company by having done it yourself. That way you can accurately judge a candidate's capability to meet *your* needs when you make the hiring decision, and then be able to evaluate, once they start working for you, whether or not they're moving ahead and making the necessary progress.

This doesn't necessarily require you to become an expert in that field or that job function - it just requires a basic understanding of what that person is doing. You will want to find somebody who's done what you're learning to do and use them as a resource. That way, every time something comes up, be it a project to bid on or any other aspect of your business as you grow it, you will have at least one or more people to run things by to see if what you're doing in that case makes sense. In fact, having multiple people who can provide advice based on experience is the only way you can really move ahead with your project.

Take sales as an example. Unless you lead by example and train others correctly - so that your sales people fully understand what they're selling and who they're selling to - every person you hire may fall flat on their face and every outside consultant may overcharge you. You yourself must know the best techniques to sell your product or service. Only then will your employees do the job right.

Let's say you want to get an app built and know nothing about software design. You have not researched timelines, price points, or any of the other many factors that go into the process. You will then reach out to different developers, and they will give you prices that may range widely - say anywhere from $5,000 to $200,000. In this scenario, you will have absolutely *no clue* how to make a decision, and probably shouldn't even attempt it. Frankly, there's no reason to assume you're not going to be completely ripped off.

People often ask me how they can possibly gain expertise in a variety of fields. My answer is that if possible, before striking out on their own, they should go work for someone who does the thing you want to learn to do. Take a year or two to build up industry knowledge, make connections and gain experience while getting paid a salary from someone else's bottom line. Once you have learned everything you can from that situation you can go off and do it on your own.

This does take patience. Not every young entrepreneur has the constitution to work for someone else for six to eighteen months in order to build out their skill-set. However, it's a necessary part of you being able to walk away with the important knowledge base and contacts that will enable you to do it on your own. Additionally, instead of wasting capital, you'll be acquiring it in the form of salary. You might as well have somebody pay you while you're learning about their industry.

My "know before you go" philosophy on hiring reaches both high and low. You will need people to mentor you in a specific industry when you're attempting to break into it, but eventually you'll be in charge of people. When you reach that pinnacle, you must be able to give direction to others and hold them accountable. Most important: you'll also need to learn how to hold *yourself* accountable. No matter how many talented people you hire the buck stops with you. You're the one ultimately responsible for the fate of your company. The examples in this chapter were lessons I learned that, if you take them to heart, can help you succeed in being able to direct others and yourself.

* * *

Section I: Learn Each Task as You Go

When I started my very first company, **Softbol**, my partner Mark Ozur and I didn't go out immediately and hire a bunch of employees. In fact, we didn't hire *anyone*. We were two young guys running a company out of our apartments, and everything fell on our shoulders. In retrospect, I'm glad we had to survive on a bootstrapper's budget. It forced us to expand our knowledge into fields we had never previously considered.

At **Softbol**, we first had figured out how to sell my product. As part of that, we had to learn some basics. We had to figure out how to do accounting - something with which we had zero experience. We had to figure out how to collect money from clients, which is always a challenge. We had to learn customer support. We had to figure out how to work a trade show. We had to figure out how to market ourselves and generate publicity. Eventually, we had to figure out how to rent an office, and yes, later on, how to hire the right people.

Mark and I did all of these things before we made a single hire. Granted, we probably didn't do them as well as people with years of experience. However, we were gaining something infinitely more valuable: a baseline understanding of how each facet of our company functioned. That way, when it came time to recruit people, we would be better informed as to our expectations, and have some measure against which to gauge their productivity.

As I said, we put this philosophy into practice at **Softbol**. After months of learning and growing, our first onboard hire was an accounts receivable & collections person. After I had spent months calling up customers and begging for them to pay, we found someone to hound the customers until they finally paid.

Our second hire was for customer support - this was a skill we already had mastered. Since we knew what was needed to succeed in the role, we could easily evaluate that employee's performance. This new hire gave me more time to continue to learn about other parts of my business. When it eventually came time to employ people in *those* positions, it would again be with an established knowledge base on my part, and Mark's.

Look, you never want to hire someone who says they can solve a problem for you, yet you have no idea whether or not they really can. I can't emphasize enough how vital it is for you to establish at least a modicum of experience in many different aspects of your business. Don't be afraid to become a jack of all trades and not achieve mastery in those arenas. Remember, you're an entrepreneur, so wearing many hats should be part of your inherent nature.

At my subsequent company, **Omtool**, I continued implementing this "know before you go" attitude. My first hire there was a programmer. This is an area where I am truly an expert, which made it incredibly easy for me to know exactly what I expected this programmer to do, see whether or not she was doing it, and know for certain if she was doing a good job. Since I spoke her language, she couldn't fool me in any way.

This metaphor of language is apt in illustrating my larger point about how to staff your company. Say you hire someone to provide translation services so you can negotiate with a client in France. If you were fluent in French, you would have a very good idea of the translator's accuracy. If you knew a little French, you could at least be confident that they were getting your ideas across. If you had no French, they could be speaking complete gibberish and you wouldn't know. My point: always try to know a little "French."

Once I had my **Omtool** programmer working efficiently, I

was able to focus my efforts in other directions such as selling the product, marketing it and managing the accounting.
I even learned how to run the logistics of shipping out our
product. Shipping was simple but time-consuming back in
the day when we had to send all our products out on floppy
disks. After learning those shipping ins and outs, I hired
someone to take care of shipping and handling so that I could
focus my efforts elsewhere.

I repeated this process with all my different departments
at **Omtool**. I didn't view my strategy as slowing **Omtool**'s
growth - I viewed it as creating sustainable growth and a
culture of mutual respect. That's always been vital to how I
do business, and to how I run the day-to-day operations that
can make or break a company. I did this years before the TV
show "Undercover Boss." I wasn't undercover, but there's a
similar principle involved.

Don't Be Afraid of Doing a Miserable Job

As you dip your toes into this cornucopia of new skill-sets,
you are going to stumble along the way. You'll find that you
naturally take to some tasks, while others prove more difficult, perhaps even incomprehensible. The important thing
is continuing to forge ahead in educating yourself no matter
how foolish or incapable your efforts might make you feel.

In the early 1980s, during the halcyon days of **Softbol**, I
had the opportunity to meet with a large Japanese computer
conglomerate called NEC that sold their products in the United States. One of their sales reps, who had worked with me
at that summer job at Cortex, got me an appointment with
them. My goal was to try to convince NEC to give me a free
computer, which would allow me to get the **Softbol** convert-

er working on their computers. If I could do that, maybe we could stumble into an opportunity to work with them, and that would help grow the business.

Remember, back then I was still young, and much more comfortable programming than pitching in meetings. I had never before been in front of a customer on this level, much less able to convince a business person to give me something for free. In this case, I was flying solo – Mark didn't join me in this meeting. As I entered the meeting to discuss my ideas, I was greeted by an audience of five suited businessmen, all seated around a coffee table. I was so nervous that the moment I launched into my presentation, my coffee cup slipped out of my hand, spilled all over the table, and dripped down onto three of the men's slacks. They weren't wearing cheap suits either, let me tell you!

I immediately felt ridiculous - as far as you can get from being a polished, slick salesman who could walk away having gotten his "ask." This was a classic case of me knowing nothing about what I was doing, being unprepared for the situation I was walking into, and yet - still having the guts to go for it and the willingness to learn in real circumstances.

After my initial embarrassed reaction, I quickly helped clean up the mess, and launched into my pitch. In the end they agreed to send me a free computer! Looking back, this was probably a trivial request for them to fulfill, but to me this was a huge get. I had acquired another computer on which I could build out my **Softbol** converter, which saved my fledgling company many valuable dollars.

Walking into this situation without a ton of confidence or, let's face it, a real ability to pull it off, I just tried my best. I messed up, literally. But my slip had not been catastrophic.

Even if I had left without what I came for, at least I would have gotten through this first time experience. The next time would never be as hard.

As you work your way through bootstrapping your company, there are going to be a lot of first times - a lot of spilled cups of coffee, metaphorically speaking. The important thing is to clean up any mess as you go, and constantly learn from your mistakes. Sure, you may do a bad job on your first go-round, but you will keep progressing if you stay humble and value every experience as a way to do better next time.

People Are Basically Nice

When people see that you are attempting something, they will appreciate the effort and be kind towards you. They might even feel a little sorry for you as they see that you are struggling. They'll want you to be successful, and often they will generously extend themselves to help you be successful. Never have I run into a situation where I was disrespected or rudely turned away when I was trying something out. If you put yourself out there, people will respond. They might see something of themselves in you. They might relate to what you are going through. They don't want to embarrass you. They want to see you become successful because it makes them feel better about themselves and the position they occupy in their industry. As I have said before, helping a young person move up the ladder in their field is a common desire in people when they reach the top.

Push Yourself In Uncomfortable Directions

Today, at this mature stage of my career, I am often asked to give speeches. Over the course of a year, I may address thousands of people at universities, conferences, fundraising events and trade shows. Honestly, I've gotten pretty good at it. I now know how to be comfortable at public speaking and master a stage. I didn't always possess this skill. A few years ago, as my numbers of speaking engagements really started to rise, some people I trust told me that I needed to up my game and that a good way to do so was to take improvisation classes.

Improv classes? That was *miles* away from my comfort zone. To stand in front of strangers and present in an off-the-cuff way, with emotion, was not something I thought I could do. I tried to ignore the suggestion, but for some reason a couple of months after I got this advice, I found the thought still rolling around in my head. I decided I had to sign up for the classes - if for no reason other than precisely *because* it was so far outside my comfort zone!

The initial nine-week course I took threw me into the mix with comedic actors. These were people who were taking improv seriously. To my great surprise, I also loved it. I had forced myself to do something I thought would make me extremely uncomfortable, but instead discovered a new enjoyment in life. Along the way that experience vastly improved my stage presence. Now when I jump into a networking event, I am able to connect with people on an entirely new level. These days, when I get on stage at a conference or other event, I get the same adrenaline high I do when I perform improv in an amateur theatre group - which was so much fun as well as professionally rewarding that it's still something I do from time to time.

Always push yourself beyond what you think you can do, or what you think you *want* to do. The good thing about having this mindset is that it extends to all aspects of your business. If you have the attitude of "I can master anything", there is no limit to how far you can go. Continually educating and improving yourself is a requisite to success, as any successful executive or entrepreneur will tell you. Also, the more you know, the better you will be able to manage your employees, as we just discussed.

Even after having built several successful companies, I continued to educate myself by taking executive education programs at Harvard University (the "Owners & Presidents Management" program). It was a difficult application process, and it wasn't cheap. Three weeks a year for three years I studied with Harvard's very best business professors. What I gained from that experience was an understanding of all facets of running a company - be it marketing, accounting, finance, human resources, etc., - at the deep-level of an Ivy-League education. I knew that the next time I started a company I would have an even greater knowledge and proficiency in these areas, gleaned from genius professors who imparted their real-world experience. They taught tested principles on matters which I had considered very dry, particularly accounting. By having true experts help me through the process, I can now follow what's going on when I'm in meetings about accounting matters. I can really understand what's going on, and that's priceless.

* * *

Section II: Find People Who Have Something to Prove

When you are ready to hire, it's imperative to find employees who are a good fit for your company. They should gel with the overall culture, share your vision, and be dedicated beyond collecting the paycheck. This means you also need to be adept at *when* to hire someone. You want to catch them at the point in their career when they will give you the most return on your investment in them.

The key thing is to look for people who have something to prove to themselves as well as to you. The best hire is someone at the stage of their career where they have personally committed to themselves to succeed because they feel they *need* to. This doesn't mean that they necessarily need the job you are offering, but rather that they are coveting the opportunity because they want to demonstrate their capabilities in your field and your company. Look for the kind of people who like to test themselves against challenges; the kind of people who want to discover who they truly are. Chances are, if they have that sort of fire, what they uncover about themselves under your tutelage will be extraordinary.

A true homerun for you is a hire that wants to prove they can rise to the occasion and do the job you are hiring them for better than *you* ever could. With that focus and belief, they will make themselves indispensable to your company, and simultaneously build their self-worth, leading to an even better performance. Of course, you want employees that are confident, but not cocky. You want to avoid hiring overly supercilious people who tell you: "This job is easy. I could do it in my sleep." Beware of supposed experts who promise you the moon. What that person is really saying is: "I can tell that you don't have expertise in this area, so I'm going to give you a false sense of confidence that I can take care of everything for you." There is no such thing as magic, especially from employees. Any promises that are too lavish, especially at the outset, should be viewed as red flags.

Instead of looking for experts who seem to know it all, look for people at the point in their career where they have some experience, want to keep learning, and want to solve the problems you throw at them for the purposes of their own self-image. If these people let you down, they will be letting themselves down. There is no better motivator for any member of your staff than that.

Look for Energy And Intent

As we were building **Omtool** in the 1990s, we came to a point where our sales team had reached eight people. We knew that we needed to hire a Vice President of Sales who could both oversee and grow the group. We interviewed dozens of people with extensive backgrounds in running sales departments. The position ended up going to a man who had a boatload of experience. Still, one of the other people interviewed really caught our attention. Ellen Ohlenbusch was in her early thirties and came across as energetic, committed, ready for anything. We didn't want to let her slip through the cracks, so we created a VP of Marketing position for her to see what she could do.

Our hire for VP of Sales turned out to be a disaster. Three months into his tenure, we found out that everything he had been telling us he was doing was a lie. He claimed to have set up meetings that never happened. He turned in suspicious credit card receipts that didn't correspond to the business trips he said he was on. We discovered that sales appointments he said he attended never happened. Later we found out that many of the items on his resume were untrue. He was a total misfire. After we terminated him expeditiously, we moved Ellen into his position - the position she should have been hired for in the first place, except for the fact that he had the "right" credentials and she did not.

As soon as Ellen moved into the position, everything changed. The original hire we had to fire was near the end of his career, and clearly wanted a cushy job he could just "phone in" while collecting a big check. Ellen, in contrast, was young and full of grit. She jumped into her new role with as much tenacity and excitement as anyone I've ever seen.

Ellen decided that not only was she going to grow our sales department by managing people correctly, she was going to sell a lot of product herself! She recognized that the more she sold the more we would respect her and give her more power within the company. Soon she was closing huge deals left and right. Ellen also always worked late. I remember I once asked her: "Why are you still here at eight or nine o'clock at night?" She said: "Well, there's a bunch of customers I want to get through to on the East Coast. I know if I call their office after six or seven at night, when everybody else has gone home, the only one who's going to be calling them at that hour might be their boyfriend, girlfriend, wife or husband, so they'll pick up the phone." That's what she understood, that's what she did, and that's how she got through to them.

Ellen kept up her commitment and resolute spirit over the entire six years she worked with us. Talk about the right hire! The people who have something to prove are the ones who are going to make a difference in your company. Those people will work out well because they are operating on the same principles as you: they are starting with nothing and won't stop until both they, and your company, have achieved their goals.

Hire People Who Tell You the Truth

One of my most instructive hiring stories came from an unexpected place. There was a point with **Omtool** where it was growing very fast, and it had become difficult for me to really keep the quality of the product and the customer support at the level it needed to be at. We always wanted to be at a 10 out of 10, and were at that point probably closer to a seven in both of those areas.

At **Omtool**, we were selling our fax system to customers in many different industries, but since law firms sent a lot of faxes, they really needed our products. One day, our customer support team got a call from the IT director of one of these law firms, Deb Cheetham, who really chewed us out. Her call ended up getting sent up the chain to me. "I went out on a limb to convince my law firm to buy your product," Deb told me angrily. "Well, I'm here to tell you your product sucks, and your support sucks as well."

My response? I told her I thought she was right-on about everything she was saying. Ten minutes after we got off the phone, I called her back and said: "Deb, please come in for an interview. I'd like to hire you to manage our customer support team." She told me there was no way she'd leave her cushy job, but that she'd grant me an audience. I loved her blunt feisty attitude. She did not suffer fools gladly.

At that first meeting we ended up talking for over an hour. I told her all about the company and its goals, and how we needed the energy and determination from people like her. I told her that it was people like her who were going to lead us to success.

Once she saw how intent I was at making **Omtool** a 10 out of 10, she agreed to join us. Deb had something to prove; she was going to turn around our support department, transforming it from adequate at best to excellent, and she did just that. The fact that she left her cushy job told me that a fire had been lit under her. She wanted a challenge. She was saying to herself: "If I'm going to attempt this, I need to do this full throttle."

It was a beautiful association that lasted seven years. She and I would both work late every single night. Deb was great at follow up and would always make sure that everybody in her department did their work. She would go over all the outstanding cases and all problems. Then she would sit down with me and we would talk about every issue. We worked until ten o'clock at night day in and day out, but as with Ellen, that's what it took. When you hire people make sure you know that they have what it takes.

* * *

Section III: Hold People (and Yourself) Accountable

In talking about building a company, I often use the expression: "One foot on the gas, one foot on the brake." You know the amazing heights your company can conceivably reach, and you want to get there as fast as possible. But inevitably there are obstacles on the road every time you make some progress. Sometimes it can feel like for every step forward you take two steps back. As a leader, you are constantly trying to find the things that move you forward. With your attention focused in so many directions, you can develop a tendency to avoid confrontation and just hope that things you put into place are working well, as opposed to really doing the constant checkups. This will lead to disaster.

I am not telling you to micromanage but be aware of which

things you need to be watching every day, every week, every month. Make sure you can monitor them and have some way to verify that the information you are getting is accurate. This can mean something as straight-forward as putting a procedure in place to monitor your sales person's phone calls. How many calls is he making a day? How much time is she spending on each call?

One thing I recommend to entrepreneurs when I'm in a mentoring role is to figure out the *Key Performance Indicators (KPI)* for each employee's goals. You can't measure these objectives if you don't properly define them in the first place. Ask yourself: "What early indicators can I identify to see if my people are on the right track?" If you find that your employees aren't meeting their KPIs, it is your responsibility to redirect them so that they fulfill your vision.

Defining your KPIs is also necessary when trying out new business practices. In our businesses we were always running experiments, so to speak. In other words, you may have two ways to do something and you'll need to test them against each other and see which one works best for your company. If you don't set out your criteria for success or failure from the beginning - even before you implement the ideas - you will probably end up in a gray area, without any real results. This wastes time, money, and resources. Chances are also that you will not have abandoned a bad practice in a timely fashion. The only way to avoid that is to set indicators that hold everyone accountable.

Expect things to fail. As a manager, hitting KPIs yourself will help you determine whether it's your employee's effort that's failing or your product or service that's failing. If you've already performed what you are asking of your team, say, for example, making sales calls, you know whether or not what you are asking can be achieved. If you're expecting someone to sit on the phone all day long and do this task, you should know what it takes to do it right. As you monitor them, you can see whether they are doing a better job than you, or a far worse job than you did. If they're doing it as badly as you did then you don't need them, as phone skills were not even your primary ability, and should have been theirs.

At the same time, hold yourself accountable. You can't just demand "Get me $25,000 of sales this month" without knowing what it takes to get those sales. As discussed earlier, if you go through the hiring process knowing how to do the job, at least on a novice level, you will know what a competent person in this field can do and can make sure you are only hiring competent people.

Oversight Creates Accountability

As the CEO, you need to be monitoring each employee's progress, and by so doing, create a culture of accountability within your organization. If there are no set rules in place, of which everyone in the company is aware, the potential for abuse increases. One of my early hires at **Softbol**, a woman we will call Isabel (not her real name) took advantage of us before I learned this lesson.

We hired Isabel because she solved a problem for us: we needed someone to liaison with the customers and do collections. At the beginning everything went smoothly, money was rolling in, and everyone was happy. This is when we made the mistake: we stopped paying close attention to Isabel's duties, assuming she had them handled. About six months later we realized that our bank account balance was not congruent with the sales we had been making. We had assumed every-thing was working out when in fact the opposite was true.

When my partner, Mark, finally took a really close look at the books, he found that we had been getting ripped off. We had given Isabel permission to write and sign checks for small company payments. It turned out she had been writing checks to herself. I'm sure to rationalize it she thought: "I'm not getting paid enough. I'll just take a little extra for myself. These guys are too busy to notice." The truth is that Mark and I had let ourselves become so distracted in other areas of the business that we had forgotten to properly monitor our employee. Had we been managing Isabel from the beginning, looking at her reports, and putting forth the time to pay attention to an extremely important part of our business - the cash flow - she would never have thought she could have gotten away with this theft, and probably wouldn't have done it.

You need to set a precedent in company culture and company oversight that prevents something like this from taking place. When you're starting a company, the tendency is to focus on the skills that you have and not pay attention to skills you don't have, thinking someone else is going to automatically watch out for those things for you. That's never the case. You need to find people to help you, but you have to hold them accountable and understand the metrics by which you are judging them. No matter how much you trust your employees, unless you've established metrics, you actually don't know what's really going on. You must judge everything by numbers and pre-set goals. Set your metrics ahead of time, live by those metrics, and you won't be caught blind-sighted - as we were in this example.

* * *

Key Takeaways:

- **Learn how to do something yourself before expecting someone else to do it.**

- **If you don't understand what your employees need to be doing, you won't be able to hold them accountable.**

- **Work for someone else first. Build up industry knowledge, make connections, and gain experience while getting paid.**

- **Build skills by learning from someone who knows how to do what you want to learn.**

- **Establish at least a modicum of experience in all the different aspects of your business.**

- **Push yourself in uncomfortable directions, even if that means 'improvising.'**

- **Look for people with something to prove. The best hire is someone who has made a personal commitment to themselves to succeed because they need to.**

- **Oversight creates accountability. Don't be afraid to fire someone who isn't living up to your standards.**

- **Set Key Performance Indicators for employees early on. Learn which KPIs are reasonable by experiencing them yourself.**

- **Practice until you get it right. You will ultimately succeed if you keep on trying.**

8

Pivoting:
What You Must Do When It's Simply Not Working

Even the most well-thought-out business strategies will sometimes hit unforeseen roadblocks. In fact, this happens more often than not. It's something to be prepared for, so that it won't take you by surprise. As an intrepid entrepreneur you need to have a playbook of strategies for when things don't go according to plan - when your back is against the wall.

Should you find yourself in this situation, you have two main options. You can shut everything down and cut your losses, or you can pivot. I frame this in such stark terms because pivoting your business is a major decision that should be seen only as an alternative to closing your doors. It's not something to take lightly.

When I talk about pivoting, especially in regard to the young entrepreneur, I define it as a realization that what you are doing isn't working; that your business is unexpectedly heading in another direction. Seeing everything you planned for closed off to you, you "pivot" or migrate towards another type of business or way of doing business - the only intelligent direction clearly available.

As a CEO, you need to be aware of early indicators that your business is in serious trouble. That can mean running out of money or not hitting even the smallest of Key Performance Indicators (KPIs). At that point you need to ask yourself: *"Is there something I am not aware of that is causing this failure? Is there another way to accomplish my goal?"* Most of all, if your company is going under, ask yourself if there is anything *salvageable* from your original idea.

Before we go into the stories from my career, let's start with a hypothetical example, one highly applicable to today's marketplace. Let's say you've started an electric scooter company that includes an app which allows people to start scooters directly from their smart phones. Dozens of these companies have popped up in coastal cities over the last couple of years. You've planted *your* fleet of scooters near a popular boardwalk where you anticipate hordes of tourists will want to rent them. You're confident you'll be a hit once the summertime crowds arrive.

However, the summertime comes, and sales are dismal. Tourists are not renting your scooters for a myriad of reasons. Their children are too young to ride them. The boardwalk has safety officers handing out tickets. The ground is bumpy.

You find yourself hemorrhaging what little capital you still have and are ready to call it a day. Then you notice something. You look at your data and see that the people who do rent your scooters at the beach tend to leave them at a business park about a mile away. The people you employ to collect the scooters at the end of the day are upset because they have to travel that extra mile in order to pick them up - an area you never intended they would be left at. Of course, you ask yourself: *What's going on?*

Doing a little market research, you discover that people from that business park are using your scooters to optimize their lunch breaks. They come down to the beach, have lunch in a cafe, and then take a scooter back to work. This saves them time as well as money they would otherwise spend on cab fares.

As an entrepreneur, bells should be going off in your head. If you're smart, the next day you'll drop ten percent of your scooter fleet at the business park. You're not committing to a pivot yet - you're just running an experiment. Lo and behold, every scooter is rented at lunch hour, and when you track them you see that they were used to go to local restaurants and then back to work. You realize that business people on their lunch break want and need your product a whole lot more than tourists at the beach. All of a sudden, you've begun solving a question at the crux of every successful business: who are my real customers?

Again, let's be clear: it's not yet time to pivot your entire model. You've simply identified a trend. It's one that may prove valuable but isn't yet the determining factor as to whether you will be able to make it the centerpiece of your efforts. Now is the time to run a deeper experiment that *will* determine the viability of this seemingly promising new direction. You have some unexpected customers - it's time to listen to them.

The next day, instead of ten percent of your fleet you put *twenty percent* at the business park. Once more all of them are rented. You invest some time to talk to the people renting them. You find that buzz is building throughout the office park about a new, fun way to get away from the cafeterias. Looking at other commonalities, you see that these people actually have more disposable income than tourists and are more apt to spend money on your product. So, you have in fact found a solution to a problem, whereas before you were a solution in *search* of a problem.

You dive into extensive research: you find all of the office parks within 100 miles and the corresponding outdoor lunch and entertainment options within a scooter ride of each office park. You talk with the managers of the restaurants and the HR managers from companies in each office park to determine how many people could take advantage of this service and what potential competition there will be. Soon you have a map and statistics to determine how big this market could be, which restaurants and office park businesses will help you co-market, and identify the next office park to pursue.

Now it's time to pivot your business. Abandon the boardwalk to fully refocus your efforts toward office parks. You aren't going in clueless: you've got hard data to back up your move. And truly it's the only move you can make besides shutting down your business, so you need to be decisive and put all your efforts behind this change. That is the essence of a successful pivot.

In this situation, as in all others that require a pivot, you need to learn from the situation that's presenting itself. Instead of shutting down your business, you will need to make the mental leap that allows you to accept that what you thought would happen didn't, but that now something more exciting is happening - or at least something with the potential to save your business. First, build a mental image of what is really going on. Once you've identified your new data points, determine if and how you can implement them.

If you can pivot, throw all your weight behind the pivot. If you can't, it's time to "fail" and move on. However, this chapter is not about failure: it's about coming back from the brink and saving your business. My own career has been filled with many such moments. I hope you can learn from them and apply these to your own endeavors.

* * *

Section I: Determine If A Pivot Is Possible

Before radically altering the direction of your business, you need to ascertain whether a new approach is feasible. Research, experimentation, and listening to your customers will give you the information you can use to chart a new course. If you don't understand where you're headed and how you're about to solve a different problem for your customers, there is no reason to think that your pivot will be successful.

At our email-to-fax company **Omtool**, my partner Bob and I let hard data and customer feedback inform all our decisions. Our initial business model had us trying to sell our product to resellers who primarily sell and service customers within 50 miles of their office. These resellers worked directly with their customers - usually companies with twenty to thirty employees - to install computers equipped with fax software. Often the resellers had established business relationships with our competitors, who were pushing their own digital fax technologies.

Omtool's product was inexpensive, efficient, and powerful, with best-of-market capabilities. Nonetheless, in many cases, local resellers declined to carry it. "We're already selling a similar software," they said. "Even though you're telling me what you have is better and cheaper, I'm already familiar with the other product and I'm not about to switch." We also found that the reseller market was basically sewn-up by our two biggest competitors. The resellers had effectively formed a barrier between us and the customers, and we had no way to incentivize those resellers to carry our product. Their customers trusted their expertise and it was too expensive to use our sales people to try to educate them. As long as we continued to compete with *this* business model, there was apparently no way to break through the wall these resellers had erected.

What happened was completely unexpected: individual companies were responding to our ads that were meant to attract the resellers. Since we didn't have any resellers, we could not refer the inquiring company to a local reseller. We had no choice but to sell to these individual companies directly.

However, these customers were not geographically close. We could not simply drive to their offices, demonstrate what we had, and loan them some equipment to test out our solution. Of course, we also could not afford to send complex hardware worth hundreds of dollars out to every company who wanted a simple demo. At the same time, there was no way a customer would buy something from us without testing it out. Unfortunately, we had to walk away from that kind of potential sales.

This frustrated our sales people so much. They had found a viable lead, got the customer interested in our product, and then couldn't demo it. They were losing sales because of this. That affected their moral *and* their monthly paycheck.

One of the sales people pleaded with us to loan the equipment to this one potential customer. It was a large law firm and they supposedly could be trusted. We agreed, but we said we needed something from the customer first – some proof that they would either buy the product or send back the complex hardware.

We compromised with the sales rep: "Get us some commitment from the customer to buy if it meets their needs, and if they don't like it, they can send everything back and owe us nothing." She convinced the customer to get us a purchase order; we packaged everything up and shipped it to the customer. Thirty days later, waiting in our mailbox was their check. They paid. And that "compromise" with our sales rep worked.

Now it was time to actually run an experiment. Several other sales people said they too had customers that wanted to test our solution, including an IT director of a Boston hospital, and another from the IT department in the Pittsburgh division of Dow Chemical. Both were extremely interested in the unique features our product offered.

We told our salespeople to tell these IT heads that if they gave us a purchase order, they could use our product on a trial basis. We included an invoice with the product, due in 30 days. If they liked it, they pay. If they didn't, they would send back the product and we would cancel the invoice, no questions asked. We knew that once they were using our product in their office it would become indispensable to them and they would never return it. That would make the invoice payable, and our company would be making money.

Both companies, the chemical manufacturer and the hospital, agreed to this offer. Both of them did love the product and did pay their invoices after thirty days. However, we made sure our sales people saw these deals as an experiment, not as standard company protocol. Reading this, you might be thinking: Aha, this is the moment **Omtool** pivoted! Not quite. We hadn't actually even *begun* to pivot. We were still determining whether we *could* pivot. We were running experiments and gathering information, trying anything we could. Luckily this "pay after thirty days" method did start working and our sales people began coming to me and asking: *Can we try it again? Please let us try it again.* We allowed more and more exceptions to go through, because we saw a successful pattern emerging.

The next month nine out of the ten "test" invoices we sent out were paid. The month after that twenty-three out of twenty-five were paid. Now the pattern was undeniable, and we finally had enough information to determine that a pivot was not only possible but necessary and profitable. Then, and only then, did we "pivot" our sales strategy fully in this new direction.

Once you decide that it's possible to pivot, it's important to go all-in on your decision. We gave new marching orders to both the Sales Department and the Customer Service Department, and of course changed our marketing.

Our new protocol was that we would:

1. sell directly to the end user,
2. establish a general policy of a thirty-day money-back guarantee, and
3. maintain high levels of customer service once they had the product.

In short: we would do everything possible to get the product to customers and do everything we could to make sure they didn't return it. Our new business model was based on selling a lot and keeping our return rate low.

With **Omtool**, we were able to pivot because we were selling a superior product. Our product had better features and was less expensive than our competitors' offerings. As long as we could keep getting around the reseller blockade and get directly through to the customer, there was no reason why we couldn't win the sale. After we demonstrated to ourselves that this new approach would work through repeated successful experiments, we pivoted the company and saw great sales.

This also had a secondary effect. Because we were now in direct contact with customers, we could listen to their concerns. Often, they would tell us that they wanted a new feature, and we would ask ourselves: *Is it worth building this feature in order to acquire this customer?* Sometimes it was - especially if the request came from large accounts. This allowed our engineering department to create new features that modified the product in accordance with what the particular customer wanted. Our competitors were not able to do this because the competitors' customers were talking to *resellers.* We could make decisions and positive changes and improvements much faster our way, talking directly to the customers themselves!

Our ability to adapt on the fly led us to larger and larger customers. After about a year of using this method, we were selling to Fortune 500 companies. They had extremely specific needs and could pay for those needs. It was worth investing our engineering efforts in a deal that, for example, was potentially worth a million dollars. That started happening on a regular basis with Boeing, Merrill Lynch, JP Morgan Chase, and Dell Computer. Not exactly small players! But by this point we weren't so small either.

Eventually, we were able to take **Omtool** public on NAS-DAQ. The ability to pivot allowed us to become extremely successful. Keep in mind though that we were only able to pivot because we had first determined that this was possible through our research and experimentation, which opened up a world of possibilities.

* * *

Section II: Don't Be Afraid to Reinvent Everything

A point that needs to be hammered home when talking about pivoting is that you must be *fearless* in reinventing your company to address the real needs of your customer. Allow your customers to move you in the direction you should be going, then trim every bit of fat along the way. Also, when your customers let you know about a real pain point, as they did in this case, you need to pivot your entire company towards addressing that pain.

With **Omtool**, once our product was filling a need, we simply had to change our marketing and sales support strategy. That wasn't the case with another company, **McGruff Safeguard**, where my partners Gennady Linatser, Dave Spector and I had to adjust our business to an unmet market need. In that case we had to reinvent our product along with the marketing and sales. In essence we had to reinvent *everything*. It was a true 180-degree pivot, and I'll show you how we did it. It's not for the faint of heart, but you wouldn't be an entrepreneur if you had a faint heart!

This particular company started as **IMbrella**, and I discussed it at length for you in Chapter 4. Again, the software was initially geared toward monitoring the instant messages (IMs) of employees of medium to large size businesses. We knew there was a pain – we experienced that pain at **Omtool** where a sales person was irresponsible. I also noticed that several venture-backed companies had popped up to offer instant message monitoring - but at a very high price. I thought we could do it better and cheaper, thus making it more palatable for companies to buy.

We built out the platform, hired salespeople, marketed directly to businesses, and got a lot of people to try our software. We were generating about $30,000 a month, which was breakeven, but we were not growing. It wasn't because the product didn't work. It did. The reason for the poor result was that companies didn't feel that monitoring instant messaging was important enough to spend money on. Meantime, we tried different sales people, different marketing methods, and different branding. No matter what we did, the number of demos that translated into hard sales never moved to where we needed it to be.

I was keeping my eyes and ears open, not quite ready to quit yet, even though I knew that at the rate we were going we would eventually have to close down. At the same time, I began getting emails from tech-savvy parents. A couple said: "I'm an IT manager at a firm that uses your software, but I'm actually using it to keep track of my kid's IMs." When you get one or two of those, you pay no attention. When you start getting ten a month, as we did, you begin to take notice. I started calling these parents up, and the excitement in their voices was palpable. They would tell me: "You are not paying attention to where the real problem is. Businesses don't care. We parents care." Hear that enough times, and you have to be a fool to not listen.

Still, at this point we had built *everything* in our company toward marketing our product to businesses. As you've learned from the **Omtool** story, we couldn't just pivot on the basis of a few hundred emails. So, what we did as our experiment was to run Google ads, all geared toward parents, and all focused mainly on monitoring kids' online chat. I only spent about $1,000 on this experiment, and we had about a twenty-percent click-through rate. That's an exceptionally high number - a number that told us we were on to something.

Given this response, we created a simple website with a form on it asking parents if they needed a product that would monitor their children's IMs. A huge response poured in, giving us more data than we had even imagined we'd get. Suddenly we had a new, unexpected but most welcome customer base. It was time to pivot!

And pivot we did. We rewrote our software extensively, keeping only twenty-five percent of the original design. Seventy-five percent was completely new material - a massive undertaking that took us about six months to complete. We were all in, because we certainly didn't have the resources to continue if this change in direction proved fruitless. However, I was pretty certain it was the right move since I had looked at market statistics. These told me that if we reached our audience - parents with kids between 10 and 16 - we would be reaching 15 million people. A huge potential market! Grabbing a significant share of that customer base would be all we would need to be successful.

We took the product to market under the name **Chat-Checker**. It did start selling right away, but we still weren't getting the real sales boost we required. After contacting and listening to parents who had demo-ed our product but declined to purchase it, we realized we were losing sales to competitors whose products offered more features! Despite getting shelf-space in large retailers such as the now defunct CompUSA, we found that what was really selling was software that monitored website visit history as well as chat. Parents were not only interested in what their kids were talking about, they also wanted to know what they were searching for online and what sites they were visiting. In short, they wanted to be able to stop kids from looking up pornography online - every parent's hope-filled intention.

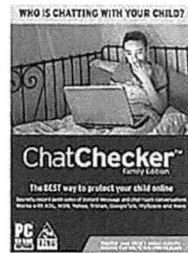

First, we pivoted to monitor kid's online chat, and we named the product based on the main feature of the product.

We soon realized that if we wanted to compete in this marketplace, we would have to build in these technologies as well. This wasn't so much a new pivot - it was fulfilling the requirements of the *initial* pivot. At least now we were competing for a viable customer base, and we needed to be the best product out there.

We did build out these added features, and after doing this we realized that our initial product name, **ChatChecker**, was no longer appropriate. We needed something with more value: something that fully communicated the brand identity and would resonate with parents. Our first effort was called **Parents on Patrol**. It had a great set of technologies, sending parents proactive notifications about what their kids were up to online. They might get an email from us with this kind of cautionary message: *Your child has searched keywords indicating they have an interest in drugs. You better take care of this tonight.* The sooner we could get them the information, the sooner we would have addressed their pain and fear, which was the backbone of our sales pitch.

We really built out every imaginable feature. We had gone as deep as we could go in terms of making a perfect product. Nonetheless, we still felt that we did not have enough brand recognition. Plus, we were competing with a company called

Net Nanny, which was almost a household name. We needed a better brand - one that people would trust. Police departments and public safety came to mind. In fact, we decided, what better brand to partner up with than the National Crime Prevention Council's "McGruff the Crime Dog!" This popular initiative combined safety, children, and a well-known character. We saw this potential collaboration as a homerun.

It took us about a year to convince NCPC to do business with us, during which we kept the company running, just breaking even from our sales, but knowing we had a final goal in mind. Once we were able to set up this partnership and had created the entity, we renamed the company **McGruff Safeguard**. Our pivot was finally complete.

Once we acquired rights to use the McGruff "Take a bite out of crime" brand exclusively in the digital world, we renamed the product McGruff SafeGuard and added every feature a parent could want.

Our company then barely resembled the one we had begun with - a company that was four names ago! We had gone from marketing an instant message monitor for businesses to an online chat monitor for parents, to, finally, a total home online security system for the household - backed by everyone's favorite crime-fighting dog.

We had reinvented our product to the point where we

were seeing real tangible success. It had taken us a few years and a boatload of effort, but in the end, it heartily paid off. Within a year of becoming **McGruff Safeguard**, we had established relationships with new social media companies like Myspace, and had tens of thousands of parents using our product year after year after year.

If you have a trail to follow, don't be afraid to follow it as far as it leads. Once you've pivoted, your new company may no longer resemble your old one in any way, shape, or form. Embrace that change. It may just be the key to your success.

* * *

Section III: Understand the Market You're Pivoting Towards

By now you're familiar with the particulars of my company **Softbol**, and the realities of the computer marketplace at the time. Quick refresher: computer resellers combined our converter with their software to sell their software in an inexpensive microcomputer. Hence, for each new client they gained, they sold one copy of our converter. Before we existed, on average, a reseller would gain 10 new clients each year. We figured cheaper computers would lead these resellers to gaining more than 10 new clients each year. However, we learned that even selling cheaper computers, each reseller still only gained 10 new clients each year. At $100 per copy of our converter, that's not a lot of money.

At one point in our development we thought we needed to find other, smaller computer resellers who were hungry and needed to grow their business. If a reseller was just starting out in his new business, that reseller needed to find customers to make his business viable. And these new resellers probably didn't have any of their own software to sell to these new potential clients. We knew that every business – regardless of the type of business - needs accounting software. Our idea was to find some great accounting software that ran on large computers, use our converter to move it to inexpensive microcomputers, and then find fledgling resellers to sell our accounting software and the microcomputer to local businesses. Sounds simple?

Back then there were lots of fledgling resellers, and anyone who knew anything about computers was helping their friends, their colleagues and local businesses get the business computerized through accounting software. We wanted to be the entry point for these fledgling resellers. What ended up happening was - absolutely nothing.

We didn't understand how hard it was for small resellers to close deals, educate their customers, and compete with the big guys. They hit a similar wall to the one we had. We had never closed deals directly with customers, such as law firms, tire shops, doctors or many other companies that clearly need accounting software. In our ignorance we were relying on novices to make what we expected would be tons of sales. Big mistake.

We had all the components and sat back waiting for the magic to happen. Of course, the magic never happened, because we were getting into a business that we knew nothing about. Selling accounting software-equipped computers to lawyers, doctors, tire shops, dentists—you name it—takes better knowledge of these competitive markets. These often novice resellers needed much more support than we were capable of giving. They needed step-by-step instructions on how to be software sales reps, and we couldn't provide them with that. So instead of a win-win it was a lose-lose until we finally shut down that project.

Sometimes you may think you have all the pieces in place to pivot, but in truth you don't yet have the market knowledge or resources to pull it off. We had neither the money nor the expertise to make a pivot of this magnitude happen. Initially we were just *hoping* for the best. Without the right actions "just hoping" is always a bad idea.

If there is one key point I want to drill into you in this chapter, it's to always do your research. Pivoting is no different than any other business tactic. If you fail to understand the market you are pivoting into, your pivot will fail. It's as simple as that.

* * *

- **Key Takeaways:**
- **Take pivoting seriously. Know it is a drastic step.**
- **Determine if a pivot is possible before undertaking one.**
- **When everything else is closed off to you, migrate toward the only available direction left.**
- **Be fearless in reinventing your company to address the needs of your customer.**
- **Let your customer move you in the direction you *should* be going.**
- **The market you know nothing about will always look the most profitable. This is a fallacy. Don't be fooled by it.**
- **Research the market into which you are diverting. Know what's needed to succeed there. Don't just "go for it."**

9

Lasering in:

Focus on the Short-Term or Risk Failure

Every entrepreneur has a basic concept in his or her mind of how they are either growing their company or hope to grow it. They have a vision - all too often a bit hazy - of where their company is designed to go, and what it will look like once it gets there. Commonly, they have big plans that are intended to solve big problems. Down the road they want to be in a position to work with one of the best public relations firms, make a splash with international partnerships, and get their name and brand out to the world.

Sounds good, right? Well, here's the truth: while it's great to "dream big," sadly, people who think *only* in these terms won't be in business very long. They would not be keeping their eye on the ball, but instead are keeping their head in the clouds. And businesses, to be sure, are not built in the clouds - they are built on the ground.

All too often, I see young entrepreneurs who have mistakenly fixed their attention on lofty goals that have little if anything to do with how their businesses actually function. The simple truth of the matter is that if you don't have short-term goals, and then hit them, you certainly won't remain in business for long.

If you want your business to move forward - and of course you do - you must maintain a short-term focus on your day-to-day operations. Don't adhere to a preconceived idea of what your business should look like. Instead, ask yourself: *What is my company's primary goal over the next three to six months?* Once you can answer this question, tailor every one of your decisions towards meeting those pre-set short-term goals. Figure out exactly what problems you can solve *now*. Don't try to solve problems that are beyond the current scope of your resources. If you fail to take care of the small things, you'll never make it to the point where you're effectively dealing with the big ones.

It may be useful here to return to our hypothetical example of the coffee business from Chapter 7. Let's imagine that you are the CEO of a coffee company, and that you've set a long-term goal of getting your beans into Starbucks. You are totally convinced that if you can break into that huge, highly visible market, you'll be a success. You also feel confident you can do so in eighteen months. As a result, you pour all your time and energy into getting face time at conferences with Starbucks' corporate brass. You make sure your beans are compliant with their Fair-Trade mandates. You become involved in the humanitarian projects that are important to Starbucks. After just three months, your CFO tells you that you are almost out of money, and, further, that your drop-shipping partner just severed ties with you over unpaid invoices.

What happened? Clearly to me - and hopefully to you in this hypothetical but all-too-common type of scenario, you were too focused on the pie-in-the-sky Starbucks plan and forgot to map out the nitty gritty of your next three to six months. You took it for granted that you were going to stay in business long enough to clinch the Starbucks deal. Meanwhile, problems with your payroll department and drop-shipping partnership were never dealt with. How could they be? You were not intensely focused, as you should have been, on keeping the doors open by paying attention to the hands-on operations that are the lifeblood of any company. Focusing on a long-term goal without achieving the short-term goals has a predictable outcome: you crash and burn.

Had you put both a short- and long-term plan into place, and then concentrated on the short-term, you might have stayed open long enough to clinch that Starbucks deal. Or perhaps new opportunities might have arisen that took your company in a totally unexpected and exciting new direction. You'll never know what was possible because, again, you can never hit your long-term goals without first focusing on your short-term ones. If you can't laser in on what makes your business function in the moment, you'll be destined for failure.

To be clear, I am not suggesting that a business *only* focus on the short-term and entirely ignore thinking ahead. You *should* think two years ahead, but make sure to scale that timeline toward actual achievable results. Say to yourself:

- If I want to be at "Goal E" (for excellence) *In 24 months, I need to be at "Goal D" in 18 months.*
- If I want to be at Goal "D" in 18 months, *I need to be at "Goal C" by 12 months.*
- If I want to be at "Goal C" by 12 months, *I need to be at "Goal B" by 6 months.*
- If I want to be at "Goal B" by 6 months, *I need to be at "Goal A" by 3 months.*

Then start reaching these milestones by dedicating the vast majority of your energy to achieving "Goal A."

Be flexible by adjusting your future goals to the practical realities of your operations. That way your short-term and long-term goals will be aligned. At the very least your short-term plan will not significantly deviate from your long-term one.

Repeat this exercise every three months.

* * *

Section I: Allow Short-Term Goals to Re-inform Long-Term Goals

When you start a company, you should have a pretty firm idea of where you want it to be in two years. Even though that vision might turn out to be up to 90% incorrect, you need to have some direction, broken down into the kind of three months chunks outlined above. As soon as you start out on that plan, you will begin to receive a constant flow of reality-based information; it's valuable data you should allow into your thinking and planning in order to be able to make all the necessary revisions. The trick is to constantly re-adjust as you move forward - always working in three months increments. You will hopefully be modifying all your decisions based on what you are learning, as you continue to monitor the day-to-day operations of the business.

Businesses do not exist in a vacuum. No matter how well-thought-out your two-year plan is, it is inevitably going to be altered - most likely in fundamental ways - through the information you gather as you begin to hit your short-term goals. Companies must always migrate in the direction their customers are leading them, and thus discover new opportunities along the way.

Where you'll think you'll be in two years often has little in common with where you end up. The longer you stay in a certain market the more you learn about it. You make adjustments by listening to customers and dealing with competitors. By paying close attention to the short-term, you will be able to gradually peer into the future and begin to see where your company might ultimately end up.

I'll give you an example of a company where we had a long-term goal in mind and then, by meeting short-term goals, needed to rethink those long-term goals, and we were well-prepared to do it. Keep in mind that this is different than a pivot, in which you are drastically altering the direction of your company. This example is about simply finding a better-informed strategy and direction for your long-term goals, and in the process building a successful business.

At a company we called **eSped**, my partners Bob Voelk, George Dhionis and I had an initial long-term goal to become the biggest vendor of special education management products. These products would keep track of each student's Individual Education Plan (IEP). We three had known each other for decades. In fact, George used to be a Director of Special Education for a small Massachusetts school district. He started his own company in the late 80's when he realized he needed a better way to keep track of his students' IEPs. He formed his company with the intention of using software to automate the process of creating an Individual Educational Plan for each student.

George needed someone to write this software for him, and that turned out to be Bob, as a moon-lighting project. For about ten years Bob would write the software in the evenings, and George would sell it. At some point Bob got too busy and asked me if I wanted to take over writing some of the software - which I did. Then *I* became too busy getting **Omtool** - a company Bob and I started - off the ground.

When the year 2000 came around, Bob and I were both finished with **Omtool**. We saw that George was still struggling to grow his small company, and we thought: *"We can pursue the market that George is in, rebuild all his software to make it professional grade, raise a small amount of money, hire people we trust for key positions, achieve profitability quickly, and dominate this niche market."*

Our software helped schools keep better track of students receiving special education; there are roughly 14,000 public school districts providing services to about 6 million students. We figured we could charge the schools anywhere from ten to forty dollars per-student per-year. If we became the largest provider, this company would theoretically be generating revenues of between fifty million and four hundred million dollars. That was the vision we had, and our long-term goal. Bob and I thought that we could use the experience we had garnered in running our last few companies to scale George's mom-and-pop type operation up to be something impressive. And that is exactly what we set out to do.

First, we decided to set a short-term goal of differentiating our business model. We had several competitors, and like George's software, the technology everyone used was fairly outdated. People don't buy based on technology – they buy based on what pains the technology can eliminate.

The pain we decided to address was how much school districts had to pay for the system. School districts needed to purchase a new system every four or five years, since the older system became outdated and the software was no longer compliant with state or federal regulations. That meant paying $10,000 for the computer and possibly double that for the software. Paying $30,000 required the school board to approve a new budget with this large capital expense, and neither the special ed director, not the superintendent, liked fighting that battle with the school board.

We decided to use new technology to offer schools a better *financial* solution to address this pain. Back in 2000, this new technology was known as an Application Service Provider (ASP); today it is called Software as a Service (SaaS). Instead of schools having to buy computers and software, teachers could access our system through their web browser and simply pay us on a monthly or annual basis.

Microsoft Office now utilizes this model to great effect, but back then this was a bit revolutionary. Our reasoning was that, with our solution, schools wouldn't have to pay a lot out of their capital budget to buy computer hardware and they also wouldn't have to pay a lot of money to buy the software. Likewise, they wouldn't have to have somebody specialize in managing the computer hardware and

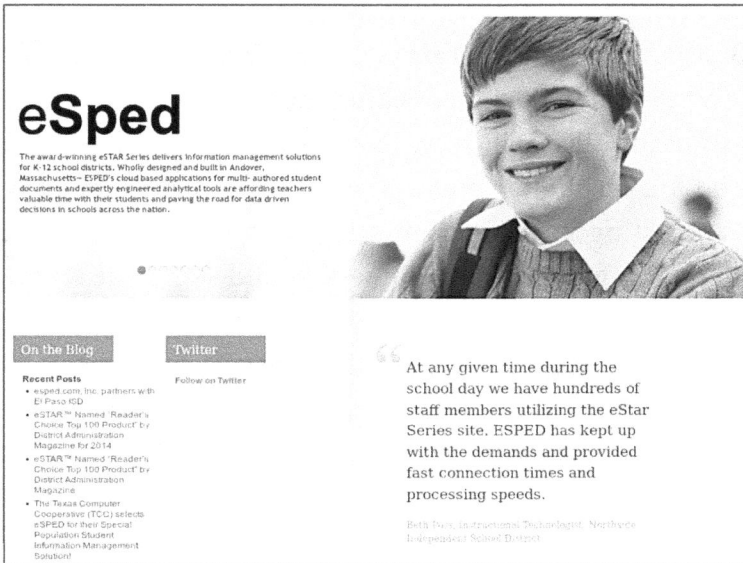

eSped's website addressed with the needs of special education directors.

software to keep it all up to date. They could simply access the software through their computer browser while we managed everything remotely.

We began to test out this business idea by going to those schools in Massachusetts that were already clients of George's. We told them: "We have a new system coming out. Instead of you paying us twenty or thirty thousand dollars upfront, if you have five hundred kids you serve, teachers can track the students' goals and progress through their web browser and pay us only five thousand dollars a year." We told them they could cancel anytime, with no obligation. The schools liked that because they didn't have to get approval for a large capital outlay. Budgets also didn't have to go through multiple approval cycles. Best of all for them, they didn't have to change anything they were currently doing. We got one school after another in Massachusetts to sign up. The company began to grow, and we started to expand to more states.

It was then that we ran into a problem: each state had its own unique special education requirements. What was required for Massachusetts would differ from what was required for Vermont, New Hampshire, Maine or Connecticut. It was costing us a lot of money to adhere to each state's individual regulations. Customers would see what we were doing in Massachusetts and say: "can you just modify that to use it in New Hampshire, because they're so similar?"

Any time we did that, it was a mistake. Similar didn't equate to a quick switch over: it actually meant a ton of work and time on our end. We were getting dragged down a hole by schools in other states that were asking us for continual changes to the software. We would end up taking too much time to meet the needs of one or two school districts in states outside Massachusetts.

Overall, we were getting pulled in too many different directions. George would go to a trade show, come back and ask: "Can we do Wisconsin?" We would say: "Yes, we can do Wisconsin, but we haven't completely set things up yet in Massachusetts." If we spread ourselves too thin, we wouldn't be able to penetrate the market properly because we didn't have the resources to do that. Even if we ended up with a great *Wisconsin* product, all our sales efforts were in *Massachusetts.* We couldn't afford to hire more sales people in Wisconsin because, for one thing, we didn't know the first thing about how Wisconsin was set up in order to be able to penetrate that territory.

Also, any hour not spent on selling in Massachusetts meant it was going to be that much longer before we could *dominate* Massachusetts. We realized that if we wanted to be a major player, we had to start by totally winning Massachusetts. In other words, instead of focusing on seven or eight different states at once, we needed to focus on only one state and dominate it by gaining at least 50% of that market.

It became imperative to figure out that we needed to command our home state before moving on. Our short-term goal of dominating Massachusetts taught us that our long-term goal was to dominate state by state by state. We learned from our mistakes and focused on one state at a time. Once we dominated Massachusetts, we focused all of our efforts on the next state—Texas. It took about four years for **eSped** to become the largest provider of special education management systems in Texas.

* * *

Section II: Know Your (And Your Competitor's) Strengths and Weaknesses

After **eSped** captured the Massachusetts market, we took the time to figure out what our next state should be before charging in. Learning from having successfully implemented our short-term goals in Massachusetts, we recognized that *which* state we chose would be crucial. How would we determine the best state? Should it be the state where people are demanding our product? Or should it be the state that's going to generate the greatest amount of revenue? We had to analyze the states and determine how they make purchases. Did they make purchases on a school district by school district basis, on a county by county basis, or on a statewide basis?

We knew that if they made purchases on a statewide basis, it would be extremely political. Was our little company, now doing three or four million dollars a year in Massachusetts, competent enough to fight state level battles - where our competitors might be hiring lobbyists? Could we win in huge districts such as New York City or Los Angeles? Did we even have the *resources* to fight a multi-year battle?

We were successful in Massachusetts because each district made its decisions on its own *and* liked our products. We had uncovered a "sweet spot" of small- and medium-sized school districts. We knew how to find those districts, get them to love our product, close business with them, and keep them as happy customers. However, we had no expertise in going after such large school districts as Chicago, New York or Los Angeles, so we said: *"If we're going to go into another state, it has to have the same profile."* We looked at Pennsylvania, Wisconsin, Texas, California and Florida. In doing our research, we realized that the one that closest matched a model we could work with was Texas, so we put our next efforts into Texas. We were able to move through the state very quickly, and **eSped** did become the biggest vendor of those products in Texas.

By achieving short-term goal after short-term goal, we saw where our strengths were as a company. We saw what we were *the best* at, and carried those strategies from Massachusetts to Texas, where we were confident those strengths would also work.

At **eSped**, our strengths were obvious to us. We knew our sweet spot was small- to medium-sized customers. We were very good at customer service, and we had very good technology that enabled us to "host" all of the technology on our own computer servers. We were able to quickly bring on new school districts. These were all small, short-term things we could focus on, that allowed the company to function at a high level while, at the same time, we were addressing our weaknesses and studying our competitors.

Knowing your strengths is not enough. You also have to honestly figure out and face your weaknesses along with looking at the strengths and weaknesses of your competitors. This relates directly to your company's short and long-term focus because so doing allows you to compete where you are strong in the short-term, gain information to try and exploit a competitor's weakness somewhere down the road, and ultimately be well-positioned to meet your long-term goals.

If you ever think things in your company are really messed up, keep in mind that your competitors are feeling the same way about *their* business. In general, you just have to make

10% fewer mistakes than they do, and you will succeed in the long run.

Much of the time you won't know right away if what you're doing is giving you a real edge up over your competitors. You do have to watch them all closely, and talk to their customers, as well as your own customers. Then you start to analyze what's happening. Ask yourself: *"What are the fundamentals of my business, and what are the fundamentals of their business?"* Sometimes you'll discover that you have something so good that they can't compete with it. Sometimes you'll find a weakness in your own business where they do much better. This is a valuable insight which can help you address that challenge immediately. Now you've turned a long-term goal of "outperforming my competitors" into a short-term goal you can actually solve. But you can only get to that point if you have a laser-like focus on what your customers are telling you, while also making sure you are functioning at a high level in the tasks you're doing day to day.

We used this approach to great affect at **eSped**. As I explained, one of our long-term goals was to dominate two markets - Massachusetts and Texas. That meant we had to fully understand the business practices of *all* of our competitors in those two markets and figure out what we could do much better than those competitors could do. In some cases, the answer was to continue to do a better job than they did at customer support and training.

In other avenues of this business, the answer was tied into our sales strategy. By that time, about 5 years after we started eSped, many of our competitors had switched to a Software-as-a-Service model as we had and were using Microsoft web services to host their software. That was an expensive way to do business, especially as they grew.

There are both upsides and downsides to using a web service like Microsoft Azure or Amazon AWS. The benefit is that you don't have to spend money buying computer servers and hooking them up to the Internet. As your company grows, you just use more and more of the servers that Amazon or Microsoft provide. Nice and easy. The problem is that those computer servers cost money – you pay for the amount of time you use their computer servers, and you pay for the amount of data that travels into and out of their server "cloud". The more you use, the more you pay. The more customers you have, the more you pay. The bigger the customer is, the more you pay.

Conversely, we had positioned our company to be able to host everything ourselves. Given that having more customers was not going to cost us any more money on that front, a

Learn your competitor's business and use it against them

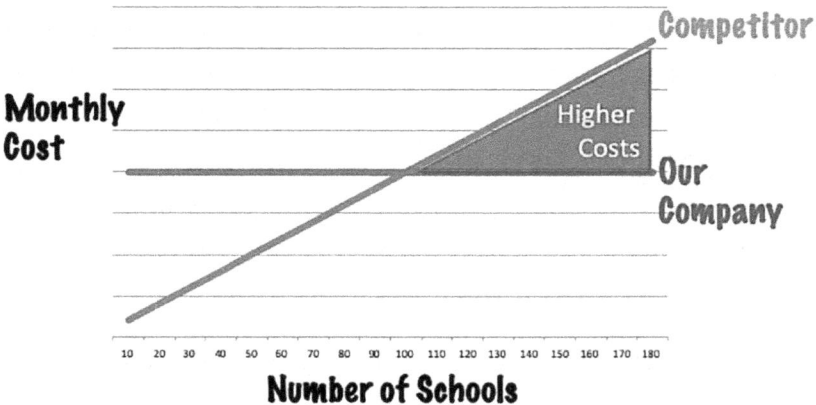

Our business model forced our competitors to lose money if they copied our strategy.

bell went off in our head, and we said: "*Wait a second. If that's the case, in highly competitive situations, let's allow the school system to use our product for free, for a year! That's not going to cost us anything, and if our competitors try to do the same thing, they're going to lose money.*"

We understood that our short-term focus should be on getting customers to do a trial with us and not with our competitors. Our only real cost was for customer service – ensuring that the customer was properly trained and enjoyed using our product. By providing great customer service, we were confident the customer would stay with us, paying for the product year after year.

Once we had Texas as locked up as we did Massachusetts, we adjusted both our short- and long-term goals. We then expanded into two more states at the same time, which we could do because now our company was much larger. We were able to do marketing and sales in two states at the same time in addition to continuing to do a great job in Massachusetts and a great job in Texas. We had established a pattern of repeated excellence, and our competitors just couldn't keep up.

We ended up selling the company for about four times what our revenue was: a great success for our **eSped** venture and a substantial "win" for all of us. This was something we deeply appreciated after all our hard work. It had also been a lot of fun. Since you've read this far, you know that having fun with a business is a big part of my makeup.

* * *

Section III: Set Metrics for Short-Term Goals

With every company we have bootstrapped, the most important thing was always doing the necessary market research before jumping in headfirst. If you're going into a new market, you need to completely check out that market. At one point with **eSped** we were looking at moving into the Illinois and Pennsylvania markets. I went to the conferences that special education directors attended and just walked around, trying to learn who the players were in that field.

To learn that, I would spend at least a couple of hours talking to various competitors to understand what they were all about, what their products were, how they sold, and what they perceived as their strengths. Then I would talk to those customers who used their products and get the whole scoop of what they liked about them, what they didn't like about them, and what they wanted to see improved. I wasn't the least bit shy in asking them: *"What would it take to switch you to a better product? Would it have to be cheaper? Would it have to be better? What are the important criteria here?"* By asking these sorts of questions when you are setting short-term goals you begin to understand the metrics you will need to hit.

Most people were very willing to talk about what they like and what they don't like. Maybe none of these people would ever leave their current vendor (our competitor), but with this information, you still learn a lot about what the competitors' strengths and weaknesses are. Is their technical support as good as the customer expects? How could the competitor improve their customer support? What do you need them to do to make sure they can hold onto you as a customer for the next two or three years? If you start getting answers to these questions from enough people, you will get a really good feel for the particular marketplace.

* * *

I want to close this chapter by giving you an exercise. Write down three short-term goals for your current business or business idea. Never pick more than three. Then write down your long-term goals. Put both of these objectives or milestones up on your wall. Whenever you need to make any decision, figure out which of those goals it's hitting. If what you decide to do is not hitting any of those goals, you really have to think seriously about what's relevant to your company. Also, if something you want to do means achieving your long-term goal before you can hit a short-term goal, put that decision aside until the next time you need to think about your short-term goals. That might be a week from now, a month from now, or three months from now. At that point ask yourself: "Do I need to update my short-term goals to take advantage of this opportunity?"

As I said at the start of this chapter, always ask yourself: *"Are my short-term goals serving my company, and can I successfully meet those goals?"* Don't be afraid to change your short-term goals in accordance with where you want to be - so long as they make sense and are achievable. Don't attempt a short-term goal that you know you can't achieve or that you have no idea *how* to achieve. Achievable short-term goals are the concrete slabs that you'll use to keep building a bigger and stronger platform as a solid foundation for your company to grow on.

Key Takeaways:

- **Don't fix your attention on lofty goals that have little or nothing to do with how your business actually functions.**

- **Ask yourself:** *What are my company's primary goals over the next three to six months?*

- **Know that you can never hit your long-term goals without focusing first on your short-term objectives.**

- **React and modify all your decisions based on what you are learning from the day-to-day operations of the business.**

- **Companies should always migrate in the direction in which their customers are moving them.**

- **Knowing your strengths is not enough. You also have to figure out your weaknesses *and* the strengths and weaknesses of your competitors.**

10

Small Budget Big Impact:

Guerilla Marketing Tactics

The point of marketing is to grow your business. I often call marketing "expensive customer education." Good marketing is about finding a set of people who have a problem that you have already solved, and then finding an effective way to reach those people. At the end of the day, you are paying a premium to inform a specific group of the public that you exist. Like any expenditure, you had better at least try to make sure that any marketing costs are worth the expected results. This chapter will help you navigate the difficult decision-making process of how and when to spend money on marketing. You will always have to spend *some* money. The trick is to not spend too much and make every dollar you do spend really count.

Because marketing will always come at a cost, its goals must always be measured in revenue. When undertaking any marketing endeavor, you must always ask yourself if what you are spending has a defined pathway to be not only recouped, but *added to.* The way to measure that is usually in raw sales, which means you need to get through to a lot of people. Effective marketing means using the least expensive methods to get through to the largest audiences. If you can push costs *down* while pushing your reach *up,* you are on the right path.

One of the biggest fallacies a young entrepreneur can

subscribe to is that marketing is some sort of magic elixir that will pierce the hearts of the public and make them love you. So many people who start companies think all they have to do is get a marketing person and suddenly customers will flock to them. They truly believe that if only people know about it, their product will take on a life of its own. The problem is that even if you let people know you exist, the vast majority of people don't care. Unless you target the small percentage of the population who *are* actually interested in your existence and tell them clearly *why* you are important to them, your outreach will most likely fall on deaf ears. The people you are reaching have to need what you are selling. If it doesn't solve any pain for them, it doesn't matter if they are informed about your product - you will just be providing them with useless knowledge at great expense to yourself. You will be wasting their time and your money. This one-size-fits-all approach is a lose-lose scenario all around.

Great marketing, on the other hand, is a win-win. It's where you spend a small amount of your own money in exchange for educating a large swatch of customers - people who actually want your product - about specific parts of your business that will appeal to them. You need to reach a large number of people, but you must target those people very effectively to make sure they are the right type of people that need your product. And you better have a compelling argument as to why they should take a serious look at you and remember you.

To begin, you need to identify for yourself what your customer base doesn't know about you. Then, to establish credibility in their arena, you need to show them how you're solving a problem that you *know* they have. Once you've done that, the next logical move on their part would be that they do listen to you or inquire about your potential solution to their problem. Until you've identified the problem you would be solving for that customer, it's premature to try to market to them.

* * *

Section I: Solve A Problem Before You Educate People on Its Solution

Never build a solution in search of a problem, or a product in search of a customer. Make sure that people who will *pay you money* think your idea is significantly important and worth spending their money on *before* you tell the world about it. You have to be certain you already have the solution to their problem before you start educating them on that solution. You don't want to educate people before you understand *why* it's important to them. Then you can explain why your product will make a significant difference in their business and their life, and they will be interested in what you are offering.

I'll give you an example from my own life where I did something prematurely and fell into this exact pitfall. In 2011, my daughter Mariel was working on her birthday wish-list, getting excited about the gifts she might receive that year. Every day, she would write out a new birthday wish-list with paper and pencil, frequently changing her mind on what she wanted and how she prioritized her gift requests. Her goal was that by the time her birthday had arrived, she would have the perfect list and would hopefully get the most important items.

She was so cute back then that I had to include this picture.

This was pretty standard behavior for almost any kid who knows that their parents, along with other family members and friends, are the ones who buy them presents on birthdays and holidays, and not some magical entity. (Not that I have anything against Santa Claus or the Tooth Fairy. They are great fun as imaginary gift-givers, but they don't go online to see what recipients are yearning for.)

As I watched Mariel do this, I had an idea for an app where kids could create wish-lists on their smart phones for gifts they wanted their parents and others to buy for them. I thought it would be a cool app for kids, but it would have to be free - for sure neither kids nor parents would spend money on a birthday wish-list app.

I started thinking about how I could monetize the app. I thought about including ads in the app, but since the app is used by young kids, I didn't feel good about bombarding them with ads.

Then I remembered that Amazon had a program where anyone could become an affiliate reseller. For example, let's say you created a website that reviews the top 10 food processors, with a "Buy Now" button next to each food processor. When someone clicks on the "Buy Now" button for the "Cuisinart Food Processor" at your website, that person is taken to the Amazon website, where they can buy it. You earn about a 15% commission for leading each of those buyers to Amazon.

I put two and two together – the wish-list app could be similar to an affiliate website. Once a kid had created a list, the app would automatically email that list to the kid's parents. Since the parent would be visiting my "affiliate" website to see what their kid wanted, I could take them directly to the Amazon site to purchase those items, and in so doing, earn affiliate commissions. The app would be free and have no advertisements.

It's common knowledge that middle- and upper-middle class parents spend a lot of money on their kids at Christmas, Chanukah, and of course, birthdays. I would be giving these parents the ability to buy their kids exactly what they wanted. I believed all I had to do was make this app popular and the business would be quite successful. I also knew that I needed to start by making the app "kid friendly".

I had two choices: I could design and build the app the way I thought it should be, and then focus-test it with my daughter's friends. The other choice was to help kids design their "perfect" wish-list app, and then I would build it. The latter option sounded fun since I would have a chance to teach kids how to build an app. Even if the app failed, the teaching would be enjoyable.

I contacted the head of my daughter's school, described the app, and said I wanted to run an after-school club for a few months, meeting three times per week for an hour. The head-of-school thought this would be a great STEM (Science, Technology, Engineering and Math) learning opportunity for the kids, so I got the green light to set up the program.

Those students and I worked on this wish-list app for about six weeks. We created slews of features I would never have thought to include on my own. For example, the kids wanted to be able to share their lists with each other. They wanted to be able to rate each other's lists. They wanted to know what the most popular toys were that other kids want-

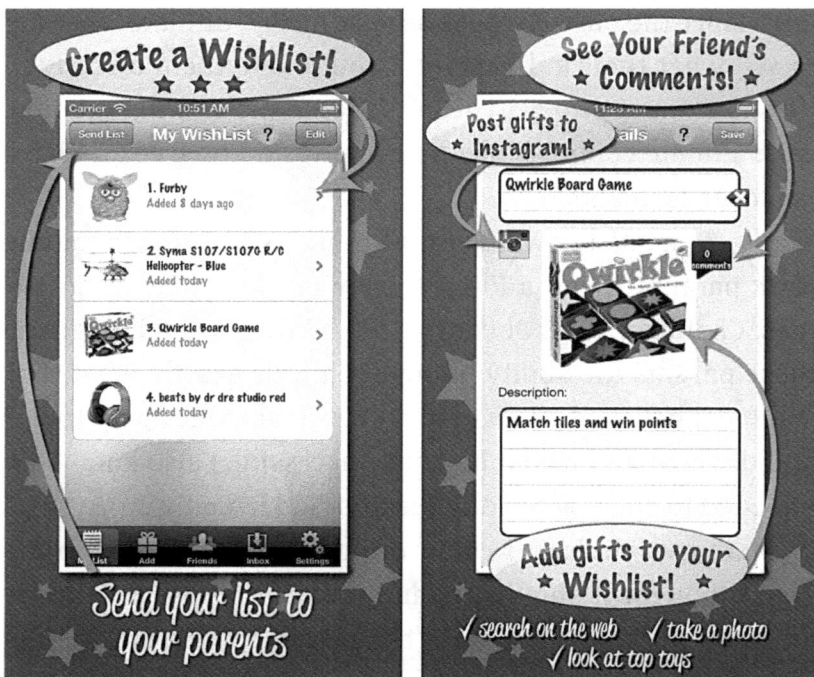

This app was completely designed by 4th, 5th and 6th graders at the Cushman School in Miami. They selected every feature that went into the app.

ed. They also wanted to be able to walk into a store, scan a barcode of a toy they liked, and have it automatically added to their list. Using my programming skills, I kept adding these features to the app.

What I unfortunately failed to do in this process - believe it or not, since I have now hammered it into your head repeatedly - was to figure out if I was actually solving a problem. Again: no pain, no gain. I had come up with a novel idea, and I had created a business model around it, but I never actually asked the kids if they would use it in the real world. My research was confined to a space where the kids were using the app as a fun addition to their school day, not something they *needed* once they were out of the classroom. I never asked them if it was something they would use on a day-in day-out basis when it was time to beg their parents for toys. I was asking too many questions regarding the *specifics* of the app, and not whether they actually needed it.

Yup - I had ignored the most obvious question. If I was truly serious about this as a business, I would have asked them: "Will you use this at home to put together your birthday wish-list?" If I didn't get a resoundingly positive response, I would have realized that the idea was dead in the water. Instead, I put it straight into the app store at the end of November. Then I queried the kids every ten or so days until January 15th, knowing that the Christmas holiday that fell during that time period would be a good litmus test for the app's legitimacy.

Out of the thirty kids in the class, only two were using the app. An audience I had directly marketed to, tailoring it to their every want, for hours upon hours, was not even using our wish-list app. The fact that it wasn't interesting enough for the kids who had built it to use it shows definite disengagement. I wasn't solving a problem. In today's analogy, there was no pain, so how could this be the aspirin!

Had I put any marketing money into this idea, it would not have had any impact. I had already "marketed" to my audience, but, again, I had failed to solve a problem for them. It was a good solution for the parents, but not for the kids who were theoretically going to drive the entire business model. And trying to educate more kids on a solution to a problem they didn't have would have only wasted my money and their time.

Do I consider it a waste of my time? Not at all! Teaching the kids how to build an app was rewarding unto itself. And it led to bigger and better things. More on that later.

* * *

Section II: How to Monetize Your Marketing Investment

Before you spend any money on marketing, ask yourself the following question: *"Will this effort simply make me known to people I want to sell to, or will it do what I need it to do and actually help me access a certain subset of those people who will engage and do business with me?"* If your answer is just making yourself known, the investment isn't justified.

However, if you are able to legitimately get people to take a serious look at the solution you are offering, and have those people *buy* that solution, it may be time to put some money into marketing. You need to market to find customers, not to educate the general public on your idea.

When you do begin any marketing effort, you need to establish this fundamental message: *I know you have a pain, and I will solve your pain in this specific way.* If you've been able to solve a problem for similar customers in the past, your message will be even more effective. That being so, you can tailor your message to say: *I've solved a pain for people who have the same pain you do. Now let me solve your pain.*

At our company **Omtool**, we created a large and effective marketing campaign through trade magazines. The pain we were solving at **Omtool**, as you may recall, was the time-wasting process of sending faxes. Small businesses were burning up valuable hours of their day getting vital documents to one another. When we marketed in the trade magazines, we had a simple singular message: "Our product will allow you to send and receive a fax from your computer terminal." Other than including the price, that was all the messaging we put into the ad. We also included our logo, which was a picture of a rhinoceros - taken from a finely detailed pencil drawing done by the artist Josef Albers.

DÜRER'S WOODCUT OF THE RHINOCEROS SENT FROM INDIA TO THE KING OF PORTUGAL AND LANDED AT. LISBON MAY 1513.

We used this woodcut by Durer from 1513 to show how much detail our fax product could provide. It was so effective that the rhino became our company mascot and imagery.

As it turned out, this detail of our logo proved to be a key component in our marketing strategy. When a customer would call us inquiring about the product, we would instantly send them an **Omtool** fax that would include an order form emblazoned with an image of this very detailed rhino. They would see that our product not only worked, but that it was able to send extremely intricate images that came to them clearly in a matter of moments. We were using our product as its own marketing tool.

Through marketing this way, we were able to establish the viability and precision our product would provide for the customer. All the customer had to do was fill out the order form, insert it into their fax machine and send it back to us. We also included a money-back guarantee. This eliminated all risk for people who thought they might want it. We were essentially having them impulse-buy a large investment because we made it so easy for them to try, and then provide assurance that it would work by guaranteeing the refund if they were not satisfied.

If you've ever looked at the prices of advertising in a trade magazine - at a time before the Internet, when such industry-specific magazines were the only way to reach your audience on a regular basis - you would see that the prices were ridiculous. A full-page ad might cost as much as $10,000 - way beyond anything we could afford. As I was flipping through these magazines, I noticed that lots of used equipment was being advertised for sale in the Classified section at the back of the magazine.

Once again, a bell went off in my head. We bought a 1/6-page ad advertising our fax system which cost about $500. We received several phone calls, and made two sales, totaling

$1000. The next month we bought a 1/3-page ad. Several more sales followed. The following month we went for the full-page Classified ads and made about 10 sales. Within a few months we were buying three full pages of advertising in the Classified section. Our company had a huge marketing profile, and the ads were paying for themselves.

Whether it was a tiny ad or multiple pages, each ad generated enough sales to cover its cost. This allowed us to conduct a very close analysis of our marketing spend. Without enormous financial pressure, because our initial investment was covered almost immediately, we could focus on what exactly worked and what didn't work for promotion. By keeping our advertising budget low, we were always working from a win.

Marketing is all about sending education out into the world and knowing that this investment is going to provide a successful return. You need to make sure you are going down the right path. Your marketing needs to be accountable to specific results - results you need to identify *before* you put any serious effort behind it.

In our approach to trade shows for **Omtool**, we implemented an extremely attractive and cost-effective plan. The largest companies at these shows would have thirty-feet by thirty-feet booth areas, in which they would use union labor to set up elaborate displays. These included carpeting, pop-up booths, fiberglass tables and cabinets with electric lighting and computer stations. These companies were often spending at least seventy thousand dollars on these complicated booth setups.

As a small bootstrapped business, we could never justify this kind of expenditure. But we also recognized that we looked rather insignificant compared to these marvels of corporate advertising. We had to ask ourselves: *How can we keep the cost of our booth low, but have an oversized presence at these trade shows?*

We started brainstorming and decided to try to take advantage of the same techniques these large companies used, while spending a fraction of the costs. Here's what we did: we blew our entire budget on a large booth – about 20 ft by 20 ft – which cost about four thousand dollars. That left no money for carpeting, booth furniture, lighting or computers. We had our rhino logo, so we thought about themes that could connect to our logo and make our booth more attractive. We came up with the idea of a safari theme. An added benefit of this theme was that we could use what other (non-competitive) vendors were not using during the tradeshow. Most of these vendors shipped their expensive displays in big wooden crates that were unloaded on site. Each of these shipping crates was about ten feet tall and looked exactly like colonial-style safari props you might see on Disney's Jungle Cruise ride.

We told these vendors that instead of paying for storage for their containers, they could drop them off at our booth and get them back after the show. That saved them money and gave us what we needed. We then covered their shipping crates with cheap mosquito netting, and voilà - we had a set worthy of an *Indiana Jones* film. Well, maybe not quite, but certainly good enough for a trade show. Instead of expensive carpet, we bought Astroturf from Home Depot. It served the purpose of cushioning people's feet and added nicely to our theme. Each of us dressed up in khakis and rolled up our sleeves - again Indiana Jones style.

We knew that if we got people into our booth with our

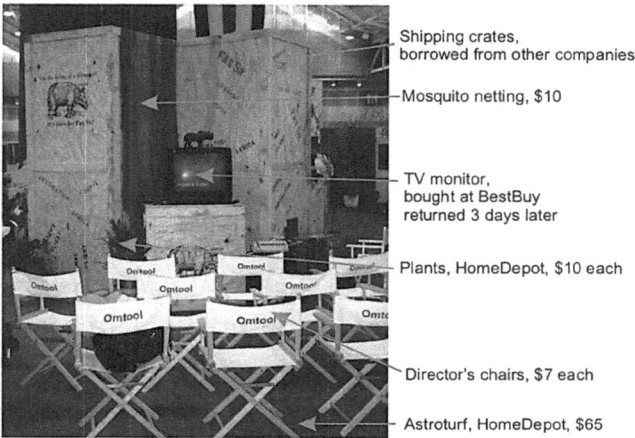

Shipping crates,
borrowed from other companies

Mosquito netting, $10

TV monitor,
bought at BestBuy
returned 3 days later

Plants, HomeDepot, $10 each

Director's chairs, $7 each

Astroturf, HomeDepot, $65

Yet another trade show done with a tiny budget. Not only did we hit our goal of gathering sufficient leads for our sales team, but we had enough money left over to give away an African safari in a contest. The safari was consistent with the "rhino" theme.

attractive theme, we could get vital information from them. People did walk in because our booth seemed like fun - and looked much more expensive than it actually was. They thought we were a large company that had no problem going all-out on a well-designed booth. Little did they know we were bootstrapping the whole way! Also, instead of renting computers and monitors we went shopping at a local big-box store and bought several computers, large screen TVs and fax machines. We returned it all after the show, three days later. We explained exactly what we were doing; the sales clerks didn't mind and were extremely helpful.

Here was our thinking about what we *did* spend, mainly on the booth itself: If we could get names, emails, and fax numbers from IT managers who might buy our product for their company, we could easily justify our minimal spend of the booth rental and some cheap safari props. If we got their fax number, we could market to them by fax, much the same way that we had done for the people who read our ads in those trade magazines. At our first "safari show" our goal was to get 2,000 leads. We walked away with over 5,000. Not bad for some Astroturf, borrowed shipping crates, and mosquito netting!

Our first "safari show" was such a success that we knew we needed to replicate it. We also knew we wouldn't always have the luxury of using left-over crates. We needed something permanent that would continue our fun messaging. What screams safari more than an inflatable rhino the size of a UPS truck? The idea of a giant rubber rhino made sense because it tied into our brand identity. And, because it was inflatable, we could expand it at the show and not bear the prohibitively expensive cost of shipping a huge sign. Keep in mind that most companies with large booths paid huge fees for shipping alone to get their displays to and from every show!

We searched the used inflatables market – yes, such a thing does exist - and found our perfect rhino, a slightly used one but nonetheless in perfect condition, for less than $5,000; a new one would have been closer to $35,000.

Over the next year, we used this wonderful blown-up rhino at dozens of trade shows. It only cost us one hundred dollars to ship, and when it was inflated to size, it was a towering sight to behold and certainly attracted attention. We did add a little Astroturf and were good to go. Costs

In future trade shows we kept costs down with an inflatable rhino the size of a UPS truck. It took far less preparation than the safari theme and reinforced our branding.

were kept at a minimum, and we were attracting the attention we needed. Everyone wanted to be photographed in front of the rhino. Visibility and uniqueness were at a premium while costs were at a minimum. As I'm sure you'll agree, this was a perfect combination for any bootstrapper!

* * *

Section III: Turn A Negative into A Positive

The night before a trade show in San Francisco, my partner Bob and I went out to dinner at a restaurant called The Stinking Rose. Every item on the menu was made with more than a healthy amount of garlic: garlic wine, garlic bread, garlic pasta. Delicious, but you smell like a vampire's nightmare for about two days.

The next day, my team and I hit the floor as usual, inflatable rhino hovering above our heads. People avoided Bob and I like the plague. Two of our rather blunt sales people came up to us, saying: *"You have to get out of here. Your smell is offending every single person walking by."* Well, I certainly wasn't going to let a little garlicky odor get in the way of **Omtool** acquiring much needed leads, so we devised a plan. I stood at a certain point in the aisle of the show, right across from our booth, and Bob stood on opposite aisle. As people approached, they would catch a whiff of our unique odors and divert away from one of us, directly into the **Omtool** booth. We were a personal redirection system. They avoided us but entered our booth!

This may be a humorous anecdote, but it directly pertains to a general principle of marketing that could prove useful to your business. Always try to turn your weakness into a strength. You might not have a budget that can match that of your larger competitors, but you might be *craftier* than they are. You might not be able to buy large ads in traditional magazines, but you might use digital marketing to your great advantage. Your competitors may advertise on television - you can divert into podcast ads. There is always an upside to any situation's challenge or setback. To overcome obstacles, you simply need to use your creativity. That's what being a bootstrapper is all about. You have to make people pay attention - even when you reek of garlic.

If I was sitting with a young entrepreneur and I had to tell him or her just one key thing about marketing, it would be this: precisely define your goal. Marketing *always* costs time and money. You can't afford to waste either. The only way you will avoid that is by having defined objectives you can effectively measure. You need to be scientific about knowing whether or not you hit your goal. Specificity is your ally, and vagueness your deadly enemy.

To come back to my opening advice, if you don't know exactly what you are trying to accomplish and are just trying to "get the word out" about your company, you'll be throwing your money down the drain. In contrast, if you have a succinct vision, defined by the knowledge that you are solving a pain for a yet to be reached customer base, good marketing can help your young business soar.

* * *

Key Takeaways:

- **Find a set of people that have a problem your business has already solved and find an effective way to educate those people.**

- **Marketing will always come at a cost. Its goals must always be measured in revenue.**

- **Establish a fundamental message that lets people know you have the solution to eliminating their pain.**

- **The only way to not waste money is to set goals. What matters are objectives, not generalized messaging.**

- **Use your product as its own marketing tool.**

- **Build consumer trust without spending too much money.**

- **Keep visibility and uniqueness at a premium and keep costs at a minimum.**

- **There is a way to turn reeking of garlic into sales. Turn a negative into a positive.**

- **Always try to find your inflatable rhino. Don't be afraid to go on safari.**

11

Let the Games Begin:

The Winding Road That Led to Blindfold Games

By now you've heard me emphasize more than once that in building a business your main focus needs to be on your customers. This deceptively simple statement bears repeating, since beneath that concept lie layers of nuance and complexity. In other words, you can't simply view people as potential profit generators - you need to really understand them in order to build a product or service that truly enriches their lives. If you can do that, your company will be able to connect with them and help them in meaningful ways. In return, you'll find them engaged, loyal, and willing to rush to your defense should you need them to. None of those things can be bought by marketing, drummed up by sales teams, or won by publicity. They have to be earned through emotional investment.

Having this mindset toward my customers benefited me greatly in the development of my recent venture, **Blindfold Games**, which I started in 2014. **Blindfold Games** is a series of audio games for blind and visually impaired people, with dozens of different types of games for the iPhone and iPad. Thus far these games have been downloaded and enjoyed by tens of thousands of people worldwide. I've personally created more than eighty titles, including casino games like Blackjack and Bingo; card games like Crazy Eights and

Rummy; puzzle games like Simon and Color Crush; games inspired by TV game shows such as Wheel of Fortune; word games like Words From Words and Word Search; and sports games like Bowling, Pong and Pinball.

I knew from the outset how important it was to treat the people who played our games with the utmost respect. When dealing with problems and complaints in any venture, I have always tried to take the high road. This philosophy has paid off an innumerable number of times. It isn't only a moral way to do things - it's a pragmatic one. Treating customers with dignity and always doing the right thing - even when there was pressure to do the opposite - has been the guiding principle of **Blindfold Games**. How I applied that principle while building this venture, and how you can apply it toward bootstrapping your business, will be the guiding principle of *this* chapter.

Before we get into the story of **Blindfold Games**, however, let's deconstruct how to treat customers in ways that legitimately consider their needs without patronizing them. Lots of corporations pay lip service to this idea, telling people that they are "more than just a number." However, when they call Customer Service they feel exactly like a number. Your messaging can't be incongruous with customer experience. That's a surefire way to engender mistrust in your business and, frankly, make your company seem hypocritical.

What you *should* be doing is treating your customers in ways that are consistent with your personal goals. Those goals are why you're spending your life doing what you're doing. Keep in mind that your customers are, in essence, paying your salary and judging your future. You have to take perfect care of them so that they care about you as much as you care about them. That attitude comes from your corporate values, listening to people, and viewing them as individuals with legitimate viewpoints.

This mindset is especially important if your customers come from a group of people that have been historically marginalized, as blind people have been. I'll admit that before I started this company, I didn't know any blind people. I now know many, and, importantly, I know about the struggles they face. That understanding and those relationships took time and effort. I had to leave preconceptions at the door and get my head around some new ideas. For example, most blind people I talk to don't think there is justification for calling them a "community." Yes, these people may have one attribute in common, but to them that one commonality they hold doesn't make them a community. To think of them that way is to jump to an unfounded assumption about them and fails to respect each person as an individual.

If you ask someone: "Are you a visually impaired person?" they will usually say: "No, I'm a person *with* a visual impairment." The crucial distinction here is that their blindness or visual impairment is not their primary defining feature. I believe this differential was best described by these statements: The National Foundation of the Blind wrote: "Blindness is not the characteristic that defines you or your future"; while The American Council of the Blind stated: "People who are blind or visually impaired should strive to be the best they can be, and we believe that each blind or visually impaired person has the right and responsibility to define success on his or her own terms."

I've gotten a bit ahead of myself. **Blindfold Games** actually began in my daughter's sixth-grade app club, the same one where I developed the **Wish-to-List** app, which I described earlier.

When we ran the club for a second time, the kids told me: "We don't want to build some lame app. We want to build a cool game." If you know anything about kids these days, you'll know that smartphone games rank somewhere between free candy and extra birthday presents. I thought to myself that if I'm going to use my programming time in the evening to build a game that we design in the after-school club, it has to be different from the millions of games that are already in the app store. I told the kids to come back to me in two weeks with some unique games that weren't simply clones of Angry Birds.

When we met for the next club, the games they had dreamed up were almost identical to ones that already existed. I had been brainstorming as well, and tried to think of ways that we could make an iPhone game distinct. I told the class: "Let's do something really different. Let's make a game that doesn't use the screen." The kids looked at me like I was crazy. I went on: "Why don't we do an automobile-driving game for blind people where you drive with your ears instead of your eyes?" I asked them.

I had gotten that idea earlier in the week, while I was at home messing around with my iPad. As I was twisting it back and forth to get the focus to be horizontal or vertical, I realized that what I was doing resembled the motion of manipulating a steering wheel. *Hmm,* I thought: *Maybe I could invent a driving game where you steer your iPad like a steering wheel without having to look at the screen.*

Then I thought: *How would anyone know where the sides of the roads were?* It came to me that users could wear headphones. If they steered too far to the left, the sound of the game's music would increase in their left ear. If they went too far to the right, the sound of the music would increase in their right ear. In contrast, driving safely down the center of the road would make the music balance equally in both ears - almost like the sound was in the center of your head.

When I explained all this to the kids, they were a bit incredulous, not yet getting the concept, so I asked a girl to stand in the middle of the room and moo like a cow. Next, I put a blindfold on a boy, and told him: "Listen to the cow, then walk up to the cow without touching it. Walk around the cow and get to the other side of the room." By listening to the sounds that the "cow" was making, he learned to avoid the girl and was able to cross the room perfectly. At that point all the other kids understood and were excited by the concept.

I built out a test version of this road game and programmed it over the next two weeks. The initial idea was to drive on different types of roadways or "tracks" that became increasingly more complex. However, the challenge was that the tracks all felt the same. Let's say the track curved left, yet what the user heard was sound modulation between their ears. They could not appreciate the increase in difficulty or the variety of the tracks. The player would just know that they had to move the steering wheel a little to the right and to the left. This would quickly become boring.

One of the kids suggested that, to overcome this issue, we place a cow in the road, which the game user then had to avoid. That same night I went home and programmed-in the cow. Once the kids got bored with the cows, I added three dogs, each at different positions along the track. From there, the game kept getting more complex. We put noisy prizes on the road that you had to aim for rather than avoid. Again, we brainstormed: what kind of prizes can you identify by their sound? The kids came up with ideas like popping popcorn, or the fizz of opening a bottle of soda, or the pouring of water into a glass.

I met with these 5th, 6th and 7th graders once a week, where we would either design another level of Blindfold Racer, or we would test it out to ensure that the game was lots of fun.

We then created levels where you had to accumulate prizes that you could use to go up another level. For example, on one level you had to feed popcorn to a troll that you earned in a prior level. On another level, we had a brick wall that's thousands of feet high, requiring a jetpack to go over it. On yet another level, you had to get sufficient fuel for that jetpack to be able to get over another wall. In very high levels, you would have to ferry your car across a lake using a sailboat. In this level, you sail the sailboat across the lake by creating "wind" – you blow into your iPhone's microphone. On many other levels we created mini-puzzles to solve, which made the game even more fascinating and fun.

Based on the suggestion of several blind teens from the

Miami Lighthouse for the Blind, I wound up naming the game Blindfold Racer. One of the first places we focus-tested it was at the Broward Lighthouse for the Blind. A girl who had been blind since birth started playing the game and was totally immersed. After about an hour I asked her what she thought of the game. She said: "*I can't wait to play with my sighted friends. I am so going to beat them!*" That's one of the moments in which I knew I had something special. She probably *did* beat her sighted friends. In general, blind people are much better at playing this game than sighted people – they have more experience attending to environment through sound.

Teens from a Lighthouse for the Blind in Florida playing Blindfold Racer.

After the focus-testing, I submitted Blindfold Racer into The App Store. To my surprise, it jumped to the top of the "accessible" bestseller list. I had learned by then that I had created an "accessible" game – a game that was accessible for blind and visually impaired people. It was the first time I heard that term.

Almost immediately, I began to hear from blind people all across the world about how much they liked the game.

Organizations that rated apps for blind people were saying: "This is one of the best games ever released." I had started out trying to build an interesting app as a STEM learning opportunity for kids in the school, and I did as good a job as I could every step of the way. If you care about what you're doing, and trying to be the best you can be, you're going to probably end up with something that's really good, and useful. That's the power of integrity.

In order to get more feedback and to start talking about possibilities for expansion and improvement, I began traveling to lots of organizations and schools that provide services for blind people. In one instance, soon after Blindfold Racer launched, I met with an individual – Brian - who lived near the Perkins School for the Blind in Watertown, Massachusetts. Brian invited me into his home. As I entered, I saw Brian and three friends waiting to greet me, with large German Shepherd guide dogs lying patiently and obediently by their feet. As it turned out, they (Brian, Kim, Judy and Doug) had been up all night playing Blindfold Racer, and couldn't wait to tell me what they liked, what they disliked, and what makes a great game for blind people. I sat and talked with them for four or five hours, having one of the most eye-opening conversations of my life, on so many levels.

There were two universal themes these game fans agreed upon as they were thanking me for building this game. The first was a request to build more. They wanted dozens and dozens of games: sports games, card games, puzzle games, action games – you name it. The second was a request that if I build another game, can they test it before I submit the game to the app store. Several of the most difficult problems in building a product were just solved by these game fans;

they were coming up with product ideas. They wanted to be involved in the product design. And they wanted to test whatever I created, as soon as it was available, regardless of its quality. By working closely with many of these people, we could jointly create some games that would evolve from adequate to great.

Over time, reaching out to people by email, I was able to gather a group of about fifty blind and visually impaired men and women of all ages and from across the world who willingly gave me feedback when we had new games to test. This too was an enlightening experience that shattered preconceptions. When communicating with someone through email or talking on the phone, the idea that they are visually impaired doesn't enter your mind. At some point, any assumptions I had that blind people live a different life than sighted people just evaporated. What does remain is wondering to yourself, after our conversation is over – how does that person have so much information at their fingertips during our conversation, whereas I would be constantly shuffling through papers, reading the relevant ones, and writing notes on others.

Anyone who's worked in this field for any amount of time has their perspective shifted in this manner. I've heard it time and time again. I went from being completely clueless to a place of understanding. That shift was critical to the success of the project.

At some point, someone suggested that I create a bowling game. One of my testers was in a blind bowling league - something I didn't know existed. When blind people bowl, they put up bumpers in the bowling gutters, have somebody tell them where they are in relation to the lane's mid-line, then throw the ball. They usually score equivalent to sighted people. I didn't really know how to structure this game, so I would ask my testers: *"How would you like to throw the bowling ball in this game?"* Some said: "You should just swipe one finger up on the screen." Others said: *"I want to be able to aim. I want to be told where my finger is, as I move it from left to right. I want to be able to flick in some direction. Maybe flick towards the center pin or flick towards the side pin."* Someone else said: *"I want to be able to base my thumb as the pivot point for my forefinger as the aiming method."*

Taking all of these ideas under advisement, I ended up implementing a version of each of them. The testers liked that they could move from a simple level of bowling to a complex level. Their feedback helped me design a great game with many different and interesting levels.

Blindfold Bowling ended up being one of my most popular titles, with tens of thousands of downloads. The feedback, almost all positive, kept pouring in at a rate that was difficult to keep up with. Each letter written to me was extremely moving, but one in particular I received really spoke to the reason I enjoy creating things that affect people's lives. It was from a man in his fifties who used to be an avid motorcycle rider and bowler. In his twenties he got into a major accident, losing all use of his limbs and his sight. He told me that because of this bowling game he was able to re-experience the feelings and the successes he had as a young bowler.

I was receiving emails like this every single day. That kept me motivated. It certainly wasn't the money. Selling games at $2.99 each to a very small set of buyers is not going to make anyone rich. As I've said before, you don't become an entrepreneur only to make money. Go to Wall Street if that's what you're after. If you're after helping people through innovation, and if you enjoy people telling you what a positive impact you've had on their lives, you are certainly reading the right book.

As I said, over time, I wound up building out about eighty different games. Most of them came from game fan suggestions. Those were the biggest hits. I had the best success when I opened my ears and mind to what the people I was trying to impact had to say. I built logic games inspired by Connect Four or Checkers; board games inspired by Clue, along with baseball, basketball, bowling, pong, and air hockey games. I also built Blindfold Word Search, Scramble, Hang Man, and even games inspired by Flappy Bird. Based on the emails I received, I knew there were as many diverse interests as there were people. When I received the same suggestion more than 20 times, I added it to the list of games to be built.

Just some of the games in the Blindfold Series.

All this is not to say that there was no pushback nor challenges. There were. A few times someone would jump on an Internet forum used by blind gamers and say that all my games were identical or were not complex enough for "real" gamers. They would suggest I was trying to rip off their community. My responses were always polite and respectful. Not only was I aware that my answers would be judged by these "nay-sayers", but I knew they would be shared over and over again on other forums. I answered each individually and thoughtfully and posted both the criticism and my response on my blogs and other forums.

Yes, the games weren't super complex, but I explained my reasoning. When I first started out, I realized that if you're going to build an app, it's really hard to get discovered in the app store. To be successful as an app developer, you need to create *lots* of apps and hope that maybe ten to twenty percent of them are winners. You don't keep enhancing the losers, you just move onto the next app and continue to improve the winners. I always let people try my apps for free before they bought them, so that if they were not satisfied, they could walk away without having spent any of their hard-earned money.

Educating people on the realities of your business is a good way to deal with criticism. Sometimes it can help them see something practical that they previously misunderstood. For example, in one forum a few people commented that I charged too much money for the games. Instead of telling them they were wrong, I wrote a three-page response explaining all of the economics behind what it takes to develop a game. Most people have never done software development, so they don't understand what goes into building a game. I explained how each of these games takes weeks or months to build, that it takes time to coordinate testing the game with testers, discussing their feedback, implementing their suggestions, and repeating this process over and over again, until the testers think the game is great. Or that every time Apple releases a new version of iOS, it will probably break the game, and you need to adjust the game and resubmit it to the App Store.

Then there are the fees that Apple collects (30% of the retail price). This showed the critics that nobody would ever build games for blind or visually impaired people to make a quick buck, and that at the same time there had to be at least some compensation in order to keep the doors open.

My response - the explanation of the economics behind what I was doing - ended up being re-posted across forums and social media by lots of people. What was the result of this transparency? More often than not, my answers were further amplified by the many game fans on other forums, word of the games spread from person to person, and some-times – but not always – the "flamer" would acknowledge what I said and offer an apology.

As I said at the outset of this chapter, taking the high-road is not only the right thing to do - it can pay off in spades for your company when you need it the most. Since I had always treated my customers ethically, they rallied to my side when I got into a spat with the largest company in the world. It's not often that a bootstrapped startup wins a fight with the App Store, but that's just what happened because of the support of my community!

It happened towards the end of 2017. I had just put three updates into the App Store for three different games: a card game, a casino game and a sports game. Apple came to me and said: "These three games are almost identical. They should be one app." They told me that until I complied, they were not going to let my updates be released. I wrote back to Apple, explaining why each game I uploaded was significantly different, and why blind people needed them to be separated. Apple's people were unmoved: they responded that I needed to repackage all of my 80 games into five or six apps.

That simply wasn't going to work. From a business perspective, it made no sense for me to go back and re-engineer those games to fit these requirements. From the customer viewpoint, every one of my users – all of whom are blind or visually impaired – and who had paid for a game, would now have to buy them over again. Factor in that 70% of visually impaired adults in the USA are on fixed-incomes. Also, many non-technically sophisticated visually impaired people have trouble with scrolling through menus. So if each of these "five or six" apps had a list of 15 games each, and most of the users can't get past the first page of the game menu, many of the game fans would not even be aware of all the variety of games available to them.

I told Apple that they were doing a major disservice to blind and visually impaired people. After an hour-long discussion they still said: "Unless you change what you're doing we're not going to let you publish any new apps, and we're not going to let you put out updates for any of the existing apps." I told them that I disagreed with their decision, and that I thought my customers would be upset enough about this to contact them.

I wasn't going to take this lying down, so I created a notification that would immediately pop up in all the games. It read: *"Two weeks from now there will be no new **Blindfold**

Games *updates and no new **Blindfold Games*** *because of a ruling Apple has made.*" Then I summarized the ruling. I posted the same message to my blog, my Twitter, and all of **Blindfold Game**'s social media pages.

The ruling spread like wildfire through my users. They were incredibly worried that these games - a source of entertainment for a segment ignored by most game publishers - were all going to be yanked away because of an arbitrary corporate decision. Over the next week close to four thousand complaints were sent to Apple. Change.org petitions were created and signed by thousands. The heads of several of the major organizations for the blind contacted executives they knew at Apple. It was truly an outpouring, and a moment of real solidarity. I've included a small sample of the responses below, to illustrate the ferocity of the response.

***

*Marty has been especially sensitive to the needs of the blind iPhone users. He has designed games in a manner that is completely accessible to blind voice-over users. He is always easy to contact if we ever find anything needs a tweak to make it work even better. I am absolutely distraught to find out that Apple has made it so our games will no longer be updated, and no more **Blindfold Games** will be created. I have no fewer than 49 of the **Blindfold Games** on my iPhone and have purchased the upgrades for very many of them. These games are all different in content, yet similar in layout, making the navigation of the game intuitive. As a blind individual it is crucial to know where something will be located, and Marty has made this so in his apps. Please reconsider the ruling you've made against us blind iPhone users with this decision.*

***

*I am deeply shocked and saddened by this news. I have been a huge fan and supporter of the **Blindfold Games** for around 4 years now. I remember when there was only a handful of games, and over the years it has been incredible to watch the number of games grow at an astonishing rate. It is easy to see that a huge amount of time and effort goes into building these games, and as a result they are extremely popular, not just loved by vision impaired gamers. I have already emailed the Apple accessibility desk expressing my anger, and I think it's fair to say that if we are going to even try to make a difference we need as many supporters as possible. We have to see that our voices are heard! A change in rules isn't a reason I can accept to be justifiable personally.*

* * *

*I find myself a bit heartbroken after reading the notice that there will be no more updates to the **Blindfold Games**. As a totally blind person, these games have been the first ones that I could find that are accessible and usable for the blind and visually impaired persons. If I am following the issue correctly, the games are possibly taking up too much space or perhaps you all believe that the games could be compressed into one app or a series of apps. Please consider that we have to navigate by swiping through each option that appears on the screen. To sighted society, the individual apps may look like a waste of space, or an excessive use of space, but for the blind, it makes playing the game effortless and easy for the experienced and the newly blind to play. I have an issue with the games that have no accessibility options, even when they are text based and could have easily been adapted for the blind. Please don't take away the only outlet of gaming we have available in the app store.*

***

Four days later Apple called me back and said: "We've reconsidered our decision. We understand that the requirements we set out for most apps need to be reconsidered based on the accessibility requirements of your users. We will let you continue as usual." A great person at Apple talked with me about the issues at length and we came up with a better way to work together. This experience also helped me establish some good connections at Apple.

I was surprised with how each member of this community, individually, used their efforts to defend something they valued. I didn't expect it to happen, and I certainly didn't ask for that outpouring of support. Nonetheless, I very much appreciated it and felt even more obligation to each person for doing so. Each person was willing to support **Blindfold Games** because each person was being consistently served by our company. I was always creating new games and improving popular games – delivering items of value - for them. They knew we were with them for the long haul. Why wouldn't they support us?

Because I always took the high road, took into account everything each person suggested, and treated each customer with the utmost respect, I had created a product people loved - a product they were more than willing to go to bat for. Had I, as the creator of this platform, had a dismissive attitude, there would never have been that outcry. The only reason each person spoke up was because I had listened to them in the first place. The blind and visually impaired people who enjoy my games didn't view me as deserving "special" treatment for building things for an "underserved population." Instead, these people viewed me as someone who created something from which they derived pleasure. *Said differently, each customer viewed my company as a customer-friendly entity that creates products and services from which they derive sufficient value.* That, I think, is the true story of **Blindfold Games**.

When you are bootstrapping a business, you have to be loyal to your customers and build trust among them. It all goes back to valuing your customer. If you don't truly value them, you should not be in business in the first place. People know which companies do not care about them and they know which ones do. Always make sure your company is in the right category.

* * *

Key Takeaways:

- **Respect and be loyal to your customers.**
- **Always take the high road.**
- **As a business, you are entering into a relationship with people, not companies. Good relationships are personal.**
- **People have long memories, and that can help you in times of need.**
- **Treat your clients with respect and honesty and they will reciprocate.**

12

Following My Own Rules and Launching ObjectiveEd

We have certainly come a long way together. Over the previous eleven chapters we've covered nearly every aspect of how to bootstrap a business from the ground up. By now you should have a fairly comprehensive idea of what it will take for *your* startup to succeed. I want to thank you for spending so much time in my little corner of the world. I hope that it has been a rewarding read.

I would like to end this book by announcing our new venture. It is called **ObjectiveEd**, and our mission is to improve the educational outcomes for all students with disabilities. We are gamifying education and using artificial intelligence – based on each student's individual special needs and requirements – to help them build their skills and improve their learning and life experience. We are focused on all students – from pre-K to 12th grade, and while we are

Visually impaired students playing our skill-building curriculum-based games.

starting first with visually impaired students, our long-term goal is to help all 6 million students with disabilities in the

USA, and eventually, millions more throughout the world. It's an exciting challenge, and our team is uniquely qualified to succeed.

I look forward to publishing an updated version of this book with the lessons we learned as ObjectiveEd achieves its mission. In the meantime, you can visit our website at: www.ObjectiveEd.com

I've had great fun building all my businesses - including the ones that didn't make it over the long haul. That's why each attempt I made to "retire" lasted less than a week. Building a business from the ground up - initially on my own dime - is what lights me up. My favorite thing is to be told something is not possible. I am always up for that kind of a challenge.

So good luck to you, Mr. or Ms. member of Generation Bootstrap, whatever your age or station in life. It is never too early or too late to start a new business venture - or as I look at it - *adventure.*

Marty Schultz

PS: Note to My Readers:

Feel free to visit my website: martyschultz.net

and reach out to me by email: marty@ martyschultz.net

You can also follow me on twitter: @martyschultz111

Acknowledgments

Family is everything. Again, I have to give a shout-out to my wife Alla, who brightens the world for me. Likewise, I acknowledge my daughter Mariel. She makes life sweeter with her intelligence, humor and general adorableness. I've had the privilege of watching her grow from a cute little girl to a bright young woman. What can I say about my sister Corinne Schultz? Despite the petty squabbles and pretending we hated each other as we grew up in a dysfunctional household, she has become my best friend. Her son, my nephew Dan, is like a son to me. Daniel has grown into a marvelous young man who, like Mariel, makes all of us proud.

I'm indebted to Alla for reviewing each edition of this book and suggesting improvements. She made this book so much better.

Friends are our chosen family. Over the years many colleagues also became my good friends. Bob Voelk, a trusted friend and partner for almost 30 years, taught me how to value my own time, understand people's motivations, and somehow managed to build great companies while I got to do what I enjoyed.

Gennady Linatser is a long-term friend, introduced me to my wife, and showed me what a talented software architect and engineer can create.

Dave Spector, another long-term friend, taught me what marketing really means, and in each of our ventures, challenged me to always do better.

Sherm Uchill, my mentor, sadly passed away several years ago. He taught me how to be an entrepreneur and learn how to do things the hard way, until it became easy. He was a visionary; he started one of the first Apple computer stores in the world. And so many people of all ages loved him, respected him and miss him.

Ellen Ohlenbusch showed me how to sell yourself, while you are selling a product. Her intensity was amazing both at work and at play.

Mark Ozur is a friend from high school who shares a do-first, ask-later philosophy that has done well for him, as he rises near the top of the largest software company in the world.

Beth Catherwood, a longtime friend since college and a highly talented artist, helped me at critical times in several companies, and showed, by example, how it's possible to survive in this world exclusively on your own terms.

Deb Turcotte matched me in how hard we worked, how much we cared about what we were creating and how absurd life can get.

Hal Berenson, another friend from high school, was equally adventurous and keeps retiring, only to be pulled back to pivotal roles in several of the behemoths of the Internet industry.

Mark Ventre always amazed me how he always got what he wants from everybody – colleagues, employees, customers, vendors, you name it. And they thank him afterwards for the privilege of doing him a favor.

John Meltaus, our business lawyer for three decades, is a friend and skillful negotiator. I'll always remember his comment when we were selling one of our companies. The buyer said: "Why are you guys being so difficult – we're giving you tens of millions of dollars!" To which John replied: "You are giving us this money? We thought you were buying our company. If you *are* going to give us all this money without buying the company, we're fine with your demands."

George Dhionis, partner and friend, always expressed his caring for everyone around him – customers, employees and family, and always tries to do the right thing.

Arni Ditri has been on the board of several of our companies, and always has great insight into problems that we encounter.

Dar Marden, **Omtool**'s first CFO, explained accounting to me so it made sense while always finding the positive side of everything.

Craig Randall, **Omtool**'s first marketing VP, taught me that there's actually a science to marketing, and showed how quantitative approaches can work.

Bill Daniels is a friend and advisor in several of our companies; he helped us innumerable times as our companies have matured.

Rick Cramer was an advisor in one of our companies and helped the company grow through turbulent times.

Bruce Evans of Summit Capital was the most supportive and inciteful venture capital partner that one could hope for.

Paul Brountas, our first lawyer, also passed several years ago. He was a well-connected attorney on the boards of many Boston high tech firms. When Sherm introduced Mark and I to him, Paul asks me how old I am. He stares at us for about two minutes without saying anything, then says: "You'll make it."

Dick Berthold, my first real manager, taught me how to solve problems independently. When I had a question, Dick would never directly answer it. I would have to go through all of the alternatives with him and watch his facial expressions to determine which one he wanted me to pursue.

Mike Lowery gave me my first summer programming job in a small computer software company, which gave me insight on how a small company operates. He was always looking out for me, and even let me stay in his home for a while as I looked for a place to live in Boston.

Bob Strayton ran one of the largest PR agencies in Boston and had faith in our ability to deliver the products that his agency promoted. He never bothered us about paying the invoices, and I was happy to pay off a rather large outstanding bill when we finally sold **Softbol**.

Steve Brotman, the venture partner who almost invested in **McGruff SafeGuard** (before the Great Recession in 2008), taught me what makes an attractive investment.

Howard Gitten, a friend and an excellent intellectual property attorney, has helped me navigate the tech world in South Florida.

Dr. Howard Stevenson, professor emeritus at Harvard Business School, taught me and 160 other experienced entrepreneurs at HBS's OPM program, how to be more competent as an entrepreneur and the responsibilities to society that come with it.

Rhys Williams, managing director of Florida Atlantic University Tech Runway, showed me how mentors can truly make a difference for startups and young companies.

Bruce Turkel is an expert on branding and a phenomenal speaker; talking to him from time to time has taught me so much on both subjects. If you have interest in branding or public speaking, read some of Bruce's books.

Jeff Meshel, who literally wrote the book (several of them) on networking. Once you realize that other people do want to help you reach your own goals, Jeff's books will guide you along that path.

Mitch Kapor, founder of Lotus 1-2-3, who once offered me a job at his company in its infancy, paved the path for software publishing companies and then dedicated his wealth and time to improving the world through technology and social impact.

Ron Conway, president of Altos Computer at the time I knew him back in the **Softbol** days, now an influential tech investor, showed Mark and I how Silicon Valley operates.

Teachers are generous in sharing their expertise and passions. I don't know where I would have been without some of my mentoring teacher and professors. Some outstanding examples: Dr. Raj Reddy gave me a job my freshmen year of college in his vision artificial intelligence research lab - where I was like a kid in a candy store. Dr. Mary Shaw taught the hardest course I've ever taken and showed me the difference between programming and software engineering. Dr. Pat Carpenter, Carnegie-Mellon University Professor of Psychology, forced me to focus my efforts and achieve my best to gain admittance to graduate school. Dr. David Klahr, CMU Professor of Cognitive Development and Education Science, advised me on how to be a competent researcher, and helped me become even more curious about how the human brain works.

As a mentor, I learn as much from the mentees as I hope they learn from me. Two that stand out for me are Matt Vaughn, who has become a family friend, and gave me the welcome opportunity to mentor him and his partners in building a tennis academy. And Brett Whysel, who wants to help families struggling with debt become financially literate through technologies his company built. In working on his investor presentation, I explained that when pitching your ideas, people are motivated by how they feel, not by your charts or facts, and he "got it!"

I am sure I left out some people who had profound effects on me. If you are one, forgive me - and also remind me, so I can give you the praise you deserve in my next book.

About the Author

Marty Schultz is an award-winning technology innovator, mentor of promising young entrepreneurs, angel fund investor and sought-after speaker. Over the course of his more than three-decade career, he has developed some of the US's top category-leading software companies.

In 2014, Marty started **Blindfold Games**, an app development company that builds accessible audio games for the visually impaired. The company's 80+ games, which continue to grow in popularity, are now enjoyed by over 25,000 visually impaired people of all ages, and recently surpassed the 500,000th download.

Blindfold Games was named "Developer of the Year" in 2015 and was recognized for "Best iOS Game of the Year" in 2016 by the AppleVis community-powered website for blind and low-vision computer users.

Marty is currently a co-founder of **ObjectiveEd,** whose mission is to help students with disabilities achieve their best educational outcomes.

ObjectiveEd helps parents, teachers and schools adapt to the new educational world where gamified education and artificial intelligence are key ingredients for students to excel.

ObjectiveEd was given the Louis Braille Touch of Genius Award by the National Braille Press and the Vernon Henley Media award from the American Council of the Blind for building curriculum-based games for visually impaired students.

Afterword

When trying to come up with the perfect title for this book, Judy and I struggled over a great many possibilities. Following the advice I laid out in this book, it eventually became much easier to decide on the right title and subtitle—the one that would have the greatest chance of success.

It started as "Speaking of Startups," with the subtitle No Investors? No Problem." This didn't feel sufficiently exciting. After going through about a dozen other choices we settled on "Generation Bootstrap," with the subtitle "A Playbook for Independent Entrepreneurship." We thought it could be positioned as a leading book for the "movement" of Millennials and GenX-ers choosing to start their own companies—as a great many do these days. The imagery on the cover was this:

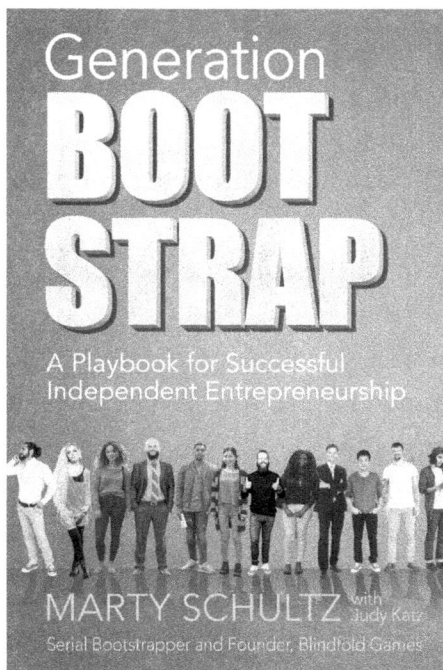

202 No Investors? No Problem.

While my small group of marketing advisors liked that choice, one celebrity public speaker who has published several bestsellers himself had a different opinion. He was not crazy about the title, and said that the cover itself "looks like a self-published book written in the 90's. Your book's content is great, but if I saw that book cover I would ignore it." So, following one of my own main principles, I created a large focus group, giving them numerous choices of title subtitle and cover designs. We came up with about 10 or 12 titles, including "Generation Bootstrap." The pool of choices included these potential possibilities, several similar but with key word differences:

1. No Money? No Problem! Bootstrapping Secrets for Success
2. The Inflatable Rhino and Other Instructive Start-up Tales
3. A Serial Bootstrapper's Playbook for Success on a Shoestring Budget
4. Bootstrapping Your Startup for Fun and Profit: Achieving Breakthrough Success on a Shoestring Budget
5. Start-Ups on a Shoestring: The Ambitious Entrepreneur's Guide to Powerful Bootstrapping Out of Your Own (Empty?) Pocket
6. No Investors? No Problem!: Achieving Breakthrough Success on a Shoestring Budget
7. The Inflatable Rhino and Other Madcap Moves: A Bootstrapper's Playbook for Entrepreneurial Success on a Shoestring Budget
8. The Inflatable Rhino: A Serial Bootstrapper's Playbook for Success on a Shoestring Budget
9. No Investors? No Problem! A Serial Bootstrapper's Playbook for Success on a Shoestring Budget.

I posted these choices on Facebook and sent it to groups of millennials I "friend" with. I initially staged the postings to just a few groups in order to ensure that the survey was reasonable and that it was getting answered. After I had about 30 responses I removed the least popular titles and posted those still in contention widely on Facebook, Twitter and Linked-In.

It had come down to these three choices:

- No Investors? No Problem! Bootstrapping Secrets for Success
- No Money? No Problem! Bootstrapping Secrets for Success
- The Inflatable Rhino and Other Instructive Start-up Tales: A Serial Bootstrapper's Playbook for Success on a Shoestring Budget

Next, I worked with Tony Iatridis, my cover designer and book layout expert. He came up with the following imagery for each of those titles:

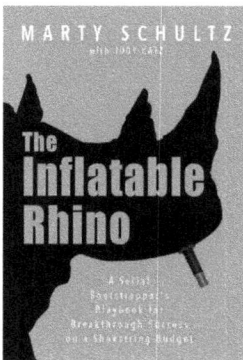

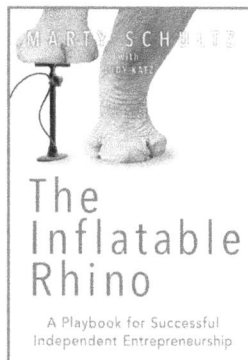

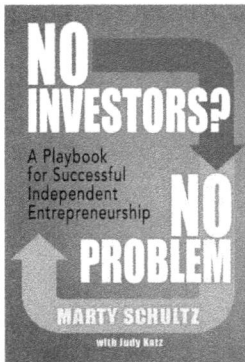

After I received about 36 responses from this new outreach effort, I saw that the horse race was tied. The comments I heard most often were:

- The "Inflatable Rhino" is a great title and will make people curious to check out the book when they see that title on Amazon. However, people looking for a book on bootstrapping might not check it out.
- The "No Investors? No Problem" gets to the essence of the book's content quickly, but it's boring.

One of the major target markets for this book: the hundreds of entrepreneurial boot camps and business schools. My rough estimate of this market is that it includes at least 5,000 students per year. I asked several people who run entrepreneurial boot camps for their opinion as to which title would motivate them to evaluate the book for use in their boot camp.

A second major market for this book: investment companies such as venture capital firms and angel investment groups. Hundreds of entrepreneurs pitch their ideas to these investors. Ideally these investors should want to give my book to these aspiring entrepreneurs when they don't think the entrepreneur's business is quite "investment ready," and can benefit from my strategies. Given this additional audience, the book requires a title that would work well for the first target market while also inspiring an investor group to buy dozens of copies of this book to give out to these young entrepreneurs so they can become investment ready. There are hundreds of VC and angel groups, so that's another 5,000 potential readers per year.

By the time I hit 36 responses, the most popular book covers were:

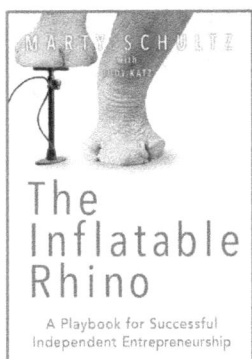

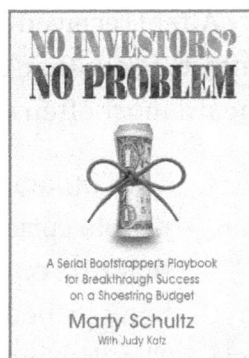

I reduced the survey to only include these choices, and ramped up the market testing further.

After another day or two I had 95 responses, with almost half of them selecting the third cover above (dollar bill tied by a string). The other two cover choices split the remainder of the votes.

Several people emailed me, stating why they thought theirs was the better choice. I was especially appreciative of the comment from Dr. Sungu Armagan, a Senior Instructor of Organizational Behavior in the College of Business at Florida International University—and a fellow salsa dancer. Dr. Sungu said: *"Definitely the third one (dollar bill tied by string). It gets to the heart of the issue and the real topic of the book right away. The first one's cover (rhino with pump) is the most appealing one; however, what the book is doing at a micro level is not clear. The one in the middle (arrows) looks old school - like it is a book cover of the past. So, definitely the third one - if you want to sell."*

The people had spoken, and my decision had become clear. Will this guarantee the success of this book that I and my collaborator worked so hard on for so long? Of course not. But why would I not want to hear back from a significant cross section of those who might buy my book before the final title, subtitle and cover design were set in stone? Why not give them a voice in telling me what would intrigue them enough that they might want to buy and read it! There is an old saying, "A man who is his own lawyer has a fool for a client." Writing this, my first book, I knew that I should not be the final judge—or "lawyer" if you will. I was able to create an effective focus group, and I am delighted with the outcome.

I hope this little Afterword has been instructive. In essence, I am emphasizing the need to do your research. And one thing more— **"Trust yourself to trust others."** As I tried to show you throughout this book— it truly works!

Thank you for taking this journey with me.

Marty Schultz

More Praise for Marty Schultz and his Approach to Bootstrapping Your Business

What Bob Voelk has to say about Marty

I met Marty in the early 1980s when I was doing some product research with his first company, **Softbol**. We met regularly and I went to their office often to discuss what they were doing and where they were. The company I worked for ended up buying Marty's company.

Not long after that, I joined Marty at his new company, **Omtool**. I was the CEO of **Omtool** and Board Chairman right to the end. We sold Omtool three years ago.

Our company **eSped** was co-founded by George (a former Special Ed Director), Marty and me, based on a much smaller business started by George. We changed the technology, moved it to a different computer platform, and rolled it out nationally. We sold this about the same time as we sold **Omtool**.

Marty is not too concerned or detailed about money. I have to help him with that, and sometimes advise him personally. I remember a time when we were trying to get ready for a major event and he went through his drawer looking for some documents we needed. He found an uncashed check for thousands of dollars that he had simply forgotten about. And we were not paying ourselves huge amounts of money back then either.

In our latest venture, **ObjectiveEd**, we are working together on something that will improve people's lives. Not only does he enjoy the intellectual exercise of making it successful – he wants to be a part of something that is making a difference.

What Mark Ozur has to say about Marty

Back in high school, I worked with Marty on buying McDonald's Big Macs to sell to kids in the lunchroom. This was the first time we applied something called the MAS factor - M.A.S. being Marty's initials. That was essentially the profit premium that we would put on top of the cost of buying McDonalds. It was a variable economic model, different for different people depending how we thought about them. Yup—we charged more for people we didn't like. Keep in mind this was high school - home of drama for teens.

The first real business that Marty and I started was **Softbol**. We didn't end up taking any investor money because we wanted flexibility. We weren't proposing to do it on our own money - we just felt it was better for the opportunity and for ourselves.

Marty is not a big fan of bringing in a lot of other investors. He is good at having one or two partners, people that are close to him with a high degree of trust. That goes with his whole idea of the bootstrap. He doesn't take on a lot of commitment and overhead and responsibility to others so that he can stay fairly flexible.

Marty believes in testing limits. You want to see what is out there, and will you have enough running room to go experiment further with that idea. I think that is an incredibly important attribute that Marty has, and it's served him well - and everyone associated with him.

What Dave Spector has to say about Marty

I've known Marty for about 15 years – we've partnered to build several startups.

We were co-panelists at a MIT Enterprise Forum of South Florida presentation to local entrepreneurs. He was the CEO panelist and I was the marketing "expert" panelist. We hit it off and started having lunch together. He told me about a crazy idea he had with some software he had written to help protect kids on the Internet.

Most recently, I was a partner in a company that helped hotels with their marketing. We had about a hundred and forty employees, and a lot of the success I've had there was due to the stuff I learned at the **University of Marty**. I got my "MBA" with Marty.

When we met, I didn't realize how inefficient my thinking was; he is the most efficient thinker I've met. You could waste a lot of time and effort doing things or you could talk to Marty and he will show you the shortest distance between point A and point B.

He taught me to look at all the options before making a decision; to test things and pursue the experiment that came out ahead and the best. He is very analytical and critical yet at the same time liberal, adventurous, curious and generous.

He falls asleep in seconds. Once our venture **McGruff Safe-Guard** was succeeding, we could grow even faster by raising venture capital money. We were on a nationwide tour of venture capitalists and we would invariably be waiting in the lobby or conference rooms for these arrogant VC's to join us. I am nervous because we have to do this presentation; we need to raise five million dollars and I look across the table and Marty is completely relaxed, nodding off.

What Deb Cheetham has to say about Marty

I met Marty in 1996 when he convinced me to join the team at **Omtool**.

I have fifteen years of emails between Marty and I, going back and forth on what would be a great product – even up to the present. If he had an idea, he bounced it off me. If I wanted to try something, I bounced it off him. We had this mutual understanding where sometimes things just take off and sometimes things die on the table after our discussions.

He is the perfect person to work through logistics of getting something to market. I am more of the person who can tell you what the market can withstand from a customer perspective. I'm good at knowing what they are willing to pay and what features a customer will demand. That is exactly how our relationship started and how it still exists today.

As I discovered, Marty takes setbacks in stride and reflects on them. It was a complete leap of faith in him for me to go work for a small company where he told me, honestly, that he worked fifty to eighty hours a week. He said that upfront. He said his business was in its infancy and that he and his partner were going to take that company to an IPO. Which is exactly what we all did!

Marty wants things to be fun to him. In terms of his being a mentor and telling young people that they should do their start-ups by bootstrapping best they can, I wholeheartedly agree. If I learned anything from him, it's that hard work will pay off.

What Gennady Linatser has to say about Marty

I met Marty when we were both running separate companies that provided converter software. We never actually competed because he sold his company just before my company entered that market. We became friends, and 15 years later we launched a software product to monitor Instant Messaging.

Marty is right that you need to talk to a lot of people to try to get a handle on whether a company will have a market. You need feedback from different types of people. If you don't try and get feedback from different types of audience, you won't get what might be valuable. You might be missing something.

Our partnership was that I was doing the technical part, as VP of Engineering. He was doing software development as well, but essentially, he was managing the business and I was running engineering. His role was literally going and getting customer information. Then we would hash it out between us, picking the best path for the business.

We had bootstrapped it for several years, and the company was profitable and growing. We saw an opportunity to expand quickly, so we started pitching to a number of venture capital firms and found one to invest in us. Unfortunately, that was in 2008 - the markets were crashing. We refocused and turned it into a highly profitable small business for another 5 years.

What Mark Ventre has to say about Marty

I started working with Marty at **Omtool** nearly twenty-five years ago. Then we worked together at **eSped** for nearly nineteen years.

His biggest flaw, which in the entrepreneurial world is the biggest asset, is a capacity for underestimating risk. Over-confidence in himself is a big part of it. But there is no question - when Marty commits to something, he is generally optimistic about its probability for success and may even ignore some warning signs.

Marty talks to everybody. He probably would ask people on a movie line what they think. And he is always on the hunt for ideas. Marty has done this repeatedly; he builds a business from nothing. A lot of people can come in and see a company with a half a million or a million dollars in revenue and take it from there, right? What Marty does is create out of thin air businesses that will generate revenue, and he has done that multiple times successfully.

For Marty there are no failures, only learning opportunities, and finding better ways to do things.

What Ellen Ohlenbusch has to say about Marty

I have known Marty for over twenty years. I was brought on at **Omtool** as the first senior executive that he and Bob hired when they partnered. My resume didn't have the business school and MBA credentials. Within about three months of hiring someone else for the position who had the credentials, they came back and asked if I would consider interviewing for that job again.

We took the company from just over seven hundred thousand to over thirty-eight million in revenue. Some years later it went public.

Bootstrapping takes time and a willingness to put a lot of time and energy and focus into something. We would work eighty hours a week and then cycle a hundred miles on a Saturday and then another twenty to fifty on Sunday with a different group of people.

You do that because you need the release. You come out of a week where there are a lot of moving parts and a lot of people depending on you. Often times, you come in on a Saturday morning and go to your desk to catch up while no one else is there. And then you end up focused on one thing and still can't clear the desk.

Getting investment money early-on costs you an arm and a leg and typically also control. At the end of the day, if you grow the business to a reasonable size, you are going to get your expectations met. Also, bootstrapping is fun.

Marty will always be your wingman. If you are working on a project until eleven o'clock at night to meet a deadline, he would hang out just to make sure you had what you need.

What Mariel Schultz has to say about Marty

The app class in my school that evolved into an after-school program began because my dad wanted to get us kids involved in tech, which is such an important part of all of our lives now.

Somehow, through bouncing off kids' ideas and his own ideas it became "Let's do a game for blind kids." The after-school program ended up turning into a middle school elective. This was the start of Blindfold Games.

Fun fact: I'm the voice in Blindfold Racer. I helped my dad twice in that game; once when I was about 13 for the first 35 levels of the game, and a few years later, for the next 25 levels. The second time I had to pretend I was a 13-year-old to keep it consistent. My voice had changed a bit by then.

It was frustrating at times to work as a voice actor. My dad is a perfectionist and often it took many tries and hours of recording to get everything just right: the intonation, the emphasis. Now, several years later, I think about that time with fondness. It was my first business project and also community service project with my dad! And I derive an immense satisfaction knowing that thousands of people hear my voice while enjoying these games.

I think, from a marketing perspective, that Blindfold Games is genius because it is an untapped market. Blind and visually impaired people need these games and benefit from them. I am also proud that my dad is doing it since it means giving back to the community.

Index

Notes

www.ingramcontent.com/pod-product-compliance
Lightning Source LLC
Chambersburg PA
CBHW070924210326
41520CB00021B/6801